MASTERING

BOR*DER*LINE PERSONALITY DIS*OR*DER *WORKBOOK*

Jim Stoner

ALT-psyhealth.com

Copyright © 2025 Jim Stoner

ISBN: 979-8-218-61424-9

Printed in the United States of America by Alt-Psyhealth.com

No portion of this book may be reproduced without written permission from the publisher or author, except as permitted by U.S. copyright law.

Cover Artwork, Content, and Document Design by Jim Stoner

For

Dr. Otto Friedmann Kernberg

1928-

In the 1960s, Kernberg redefined the term "borderline personality organization."

PREFACE

Dear Students,

ALT-PsyHealth's mission is to offer alternative and effective methods for psychological well-being and mental health. We strive to enhance life satisfaction, balance positive and negative emotions, foster self-acceptance and personal growth, and align actions with your values and skills.

This workbook demonstrates our commitment to providing alternative treatment options for individuals diagnosed with borderline personality disorder. This self-help program specifically targets and reduces your symptoms by equipping you with knowledge and skills for your toolbox.

This self-help workbook is affordable and practical, offering real-world applications and results. Each chapter or training module starts with clear learning objectives. The content is relevant for overall stability and wellness. Twenty-seven exercises help you process your challenges and strengths, encouraging you to build on self-knowledge to improve your well-being and quality of life. The manual is thoughtfully designed, informative, and instructive. It is also evidence-based, meaning the included strategies are supported by research.

The workbook guides individuals toward holistic well-being, empowerment, and personal transformation. It promotes adaptive responses, resilience, and resourcefulness to address daily and life challenges. It helps participants learn and integrate self-care techniques and strategies to enhance their success. We emphasize the importance of establishing boundaries and methods for maintaining intimate, stable, and fulfilling relationships.

Completing this book and the exercises will enhance your self-awareness and understanding of your illness, allowing you to address your personal needs intentionally.

We wish you the best on your healing journey.

TABLE OF CONTENTS

MODULE ONE: Living with A Chronic Mental Illness
- Course Learning Objectives — 1
- What It's Like to Live with A Chronic Mental Illness — 2
    - Exercise 1.1 Patti's Story — 3
    - Exercise 1.2 My Short Story — 3
- Simple Facts About Emotional Dysregulation Disorder or BPD — 4
    - Exercise 1.3 Julie's Story — 5
- Focus On Borderline Personality Disorder — 7
- Instrumental Activities of Daily Living (IADL) — 8
    - Exercise 1.4 Reflect on IADLs — 9
- Managing BPD/Mental Health Options — 10
- BPD Assessment of Needs — 11
    - Exercise 1.6 Journal Writing — 14
    - Exercise 1.7 Reflection — 15

MODULE TWO: Quality of Life and Well-being
- Module Two Learning Objectives — 17
- What is Quality of Life and Wellbeing — 18
    - Exercise 2.1 Strengths and Challenges — 22
    - Exercise 2.2 Quality of Life Survey — 22
    - Exercise 2.3 Ellen's Story — 23

MODULE THREE: Factors That Impact Your Life Goals
- Modules Three Learning Objectives — 25
- Four Domains of Bio/Psycho/Social/Spiritual Whole Person Model — 26
    - Exercise 3.1 The "I am" Poem — 30
- Working From Your Core Values — 32
    - Exercise 3.2 Reflect on Your Values — 33
    - Exercise 3.3 Application of Values — 34
- What Do People Care About Most? — 35
    - Exercise 3.4 Identity Your Values — 37
    - Exercise 3.5 Reflect on Your Values — 38
    - Exercise 3.6 Identifying Life Goals — 39
    - Exercise 3.7 Express SMART Goals — 40

MODULE FOUR: Identifying Symptoms, Triggers, and Responses
- Module Four Learning Objectives — 43
- Relationship Between BPD symptoms and Diagnostic Criteria — 44
- Life Skills Inventory—Instrumental Activities of Daily Living — 45
    - Exercise 4.1 IADL Assessment — 48
    - Exercise 4.2 Mental Health Symptoms and Triggers — 51
- Responses and Consequences to Triggers — 52
- Ways to Respond to Triggers — 52
    - Exercise 4.3 Reactions to Triggers Assessment — 53
- Stress, Triggers, and Responses — 54

- o Exercise 4.4 Symptoms and Responses — 57
- ▪ How to Cope with Triggers — 57
- ▪ Trigger Response Grid — 58
  - o Exercise 4.5 Fill in Trigger Response Grid — 58
  - o Exercise 4.6 Global Symptoms Checklist — 61
  - o Exercise 4.7 Miranda's Story — 63

MODULE FIVE--Managing A Mental Illness Is Challenging but Doable

- Module Five Learning Objectives — 65
- Collaborative Model of Mental Health Care — 66
- !!! Caution !!!   !!! Caution !!! Medical Errors Occur — 68
- Cognitive Behavioral Therapy (CBT) — 69
  - o Exercise 5.1 CBT Concepts — 69
- How CBT Works — 70
  - o Exercise 5.2 Tamika's Story — 71
- Negative Self-Talk — 72
  - o Exercise 5.3 Challenging Negative Self Talk — 73
  - o Exercise 5.4 My Support System — 74
- Physical And Mental Self-Care — 74
  - o Exercise 5.5 Assessing Your Sleep Habits — 74
- Healthy Coping Strategies — 75
- Setting Boundaries — 76
  - o Exercise 5.6 It's okay to say "NO" — 79
- Coping Skills and Techniques — 80
- Two Types of Coping Skills — 81
- Unhealthy Coping Skills to Avoid — 83
  - o Exercise 5.7 — 85
- CBT and Dialectical Behavior Therapy (DBT) — 85
- Elements of DBT — 89
- Mindfulness and Gratitude — 91
- Expressive Arts Therapy — 93
- Psychodynamic Therapy — 95
  - o Exercise 5.8 — 95

MODULE SIX-- Caring for Your Physical, Mental, and Emotional Health

- ▪ Module Six Learning Objectives — 99
- ▪ What Is Self-Care? — 100
  - o Exercise 6.1 Self-Care Plan — 102
- ▪ Self-Care Contract — 106
- ▪ Olivia's Story — 111
  - o Exercise 6.2 Positive Affirmations Oracle Cards — 113
- ▪ Wrapping Up: Self-Discipline, Self-Control, Self-Care — 114
- ▪ Lifeline to Immediate Help — 116

REFERENCES — 117-124

> *If you or someone you know is experiencing mental health difficulties, you can call or text the Suicide & Crisis Lifeline at 988.*
>
> *This service is available 24 hours a day, seven days a week.*

MODULE ONE

Borderline Personality Disorder Basics

Course Learning Objectives

1. Lay the foundation for your journey to recovery by helping you gain control over life-threatening behaviors, behaviors that interfere with you getting treatment, and behaviors that interfere with your daily life.
2. Understand the definition of quality of life and contrast it with your quality of life.
3. Learn about your "triggers" and develop a plan to manage them better.
4. Learn to express your feelings healthily by identifying, responding, and better managing your emotions.
5. Focus on problem-solving, enhancing your ability to address challenges in everyday life more positively.
6. Strengthen relationships through understanding and sharing.
7. Better regulate extreme emotions that arise from frustration due to feeling unheard or misunderstood.
8. Strengthen and stabilize your sense of identity.
9. Bring all the lessons and skills of the preceding stages together to help you connect with the outside yourself, your loved ones, and the world.

Overview

Living with a chronic mental illness can be debilitating, both physically and mentally. The toll it can take on your body is bound to affect your ability to cope with psychological and emotional stress. Not only can a chronic illness make it impossible to do the things you enjoy, but it can also rob you of a sense of hope for the future.

Important points to remember about this workbook and BPD:

- Throughout this workbook, the personalized stories and fictional examples show that everyone with Borderline Personality Disorder (BPD) experiences symptoms uniquely.

- BPD is a complex mental health condition that requires professional treatment and support.

- Individuals with BPD are not "attention-seeking" or intentionally trying to manipulate others; instead, their behaviors arise from intense emotions and a fear of abandonment.

What it's like to live with a chronic illness—
Borderline Personality Disorder?

Pattie's Story

Everyone experiences borderline personality disorder (BPD) differently. BPD is a chronic condition, and if left untreated, it can be draining for those living with it, as well as their families, coworkers, and communities. Managing a chronic illness is a full-time job that requires effort and a willingness to make changes to daily life and routines.

Patti is very familiar with making changes to her daily life. Living with borderline personality disorder initially left her feeling overwhelmed because it seemed like her brain was constantly swirling with complex emotions and emotional dysregulation, including outbursts, fear, paranoia, a sense of not belonging, intense jealousy, and more.

Before her diagnosis, she says her daily life was focused on searching for answers, moving from one doctor to another, and trying various medications. This led to even more mental health struggles for Patti, as her energy was primarily directed toward sabotaging herself and her relationships with her husband and family members. She experienced disappointment and fear that others would abandon her because she feels like she is "too much" of a burden. Although it has been five years since her diagnosis of BPD, she continues to fight a lifelong battle with a chronic illness. Through hard work on herself, acceptance, and understanding, Patti is happy to say that life is much better now.

Jodi's Story

Like Patti, Jodi knows all too well what life is like with a chronic mental illness. Before being diagnosed with BPD, Jodi says she had no idea what was wrong. Her symptoms described BPD. "I knew something huge was wrong with me because of the chaos I felt inside me, my relationships, and work. I try so hard." She says she was barely functional. She felt depressed, unpredictable, and unloved.

She describes being devastated emotionally and fractured mentally. After several years of frustrations coupled with mental health issues while she looked for answers, Jodi was finally able to connect with a therapist and eventually a psychiatrist who helped her come up with a treatment plan. She took responsibility for taking control of her life. She also found forums and articles online, which were transformative for her. "I found people who offered understanding, information, love, and support in a time when nobody but my family cared what happened to me," she explains.

Jodi says connecting online with other people dealing with similar conditions and struggling with the same kind of challenges that come with chronic illness was like finding a brand-new community. It eased the loneliness and made her feel visible and loved. "I had a voice once again, and I could offer love and support to others ... I mattered."

EXERCISE 1.1: In the box below, write about how your experience differs from and is similar to Pattie's and Jodi's. What has your experience been like, and how do you work on developing and maintaining your overall stability and sense of life satisfaction?

EXERCISE 1.2: Write your story about your experience with borderline personality disorder. Then, conclude your story by sharing your vision for where you see yourself five years from now. What do you wish your life to look like?

Simple Facts about Emotional Dysregulation Disorder or BPD

Because BPD is a particularly severe form of personality disorder, those affected often constitute a relatively large proportion of the patients in mental health treatment. It affects 1% to 2% of American adults but roughly 10% of psychiatric outpatients and 15% to 20% of psychiatric inpatients. An astounding 69% to 80% of patients with BPD engage in suicidal behavior (including suicide attempts and life-threatening actions), and up to 9% of patients with BPD die by suicide (Linehan et al., 2015). For many years, childhood adversity and abuse — particularly sexual abuse — were considered significant risk factors for developing BPD.

Some studies reported that 81% to 91% of BPD patients had suffered abuse as children. However, other researchers have made the case that risk is not the same as causation and that some earlier studies may have been subject to recall bias — especially when patients were queried years later. This means the studies are not reliable or valid. The current thinking about BPD is that it develops because of the interaction of multiple factors — such as trauma in children who are temperamentally or genetically vulnerable. Indeed, family and twin studies suggest that BPD is 69% heritable, meaning that genes account for most of the susceptibility to develop this disorder (Linehan et al. 2015).

Suicidal Behavior

Personality Disorder Interview-IV: A semi-structured Interview for the Assessment of Personality Disorders. The PDI is a self-report instrument that is a valid scale. It is evaluated unsystematically by the interviewer, who can change answers as they see fit and based on observations (Juni & Retzlaff, 2001).

Linehan states that parasuicidal and suicidal behavior is a significant indicator of borderline personality disorder and, if it presents in therapy, is the first and only issue that must be addressed before therapy in the traditional sense can occur.

The SPS consists of a total weighted score and four subscales or BPD symptoms one might experience:

1. Hopelessness (HP, 12 items),
2. Suicide Ideation (SI, 8 items),
3. Negative Self-Evaluation (NSE, 9 items),
4. and Hostility (HS, 7 items).

These "symptoms" are very commonly experienced by persons who have BPD.

JULIE'S STORY

My experience with borderline personality disorder is that I have intense mood swings, unstable relationships, and a fluctuating self-image. I often feel deeply connected to someone at one moment and then reject them the next. I do this while struggling with a persistent fear that people will leave me. I sometimes want to die or harm myself when feeling overwhelmed or criticized.

I might go from feeling euphoric and entirely in love with my partner one day to suddenly accusing them of not caring enough and pushing them away the next, often with little to no provocation. My close relationships are often dramatic cycles of viewing my partner as a god and seeing them as entirely flawed and untrustworthy. I might constantly worry that my loved ones will leave me, leading me to act out in ways that push them away.

My romantic relationships always start tremendously, and I feel this intense connection, idealizing them as the perfect person, showering them affectionately, planning extravagant dates, and constantly wanting to be together. I would let my partner out of sight, and when he left, I felt very anxious. At the slightest disagreement or perceived slight from my partner, I felt intensely angry, accusing him of being manipulative and untrustworthy and withdrawing emotionally. I am always obsessively thinking about whether my person will leave me. I get jealous and want to hurt them. I even stalk them, following them across town to ensure he hasn't replaced me. I sometimes self-harm, like cutting myself, which is a way to express my pain and get my partner to stay.

My BPD gets in the way in so many ways. My emotions are all over the place, and nobody considers how difficult it is to have this mental illness. I feel empty inside and sometimes feel like a different person or that I have other personalities. I drink all the time. I sometimes forget my kids are around. I dream that I can learn to manage the symptoms of BPD better. I would love to have stable relationships and stop the push-and-pull thing with the people I love.

I am always obsessively thinking about whether my person will leave me. I sometimes self-harm, like cutting myself, which is a way to express my pain and get my partner to stay.
I feel driven by a deep fear of being abandoned and left alone.

EXERCISE 1.3: In the space below, reflect on your current and past romantic relationships in a way like Julie's. What are your relationship strengths and challenges, and what changes would you make to balance your romantic relationships?

FOCUS ON BORDERLINE PERSONALITY DISORDER

1. *Address suicidal and self-harm behaviors.* This is the top priority because these behaviors are extremely dangerous. If someone is experiencing suicidal thoughts, they should go to the hospital emergency room for care. No amount of progress can be made if a person has recurring thoughts of suicide or self-harm. This must be addressed by professionals who can provide the necessary support.

2. *Strengthen relationships.* Relationships are fundamentally about understanding and sharing. Given that a history of turbulent relationships is symptomatic of BPD, it's not surprising that receiving support from someone who can validate your feelings can aid in the healing process. This course focuses on anticipating typical relationship issues faced by individuals with BPD and practicing potential responses, reactions, overreactions, and suitable healthy responses. This might involve stepping back and utilizing the Dialectical Behavior Therapy (DBT) model, for example. We want you to learn problem-solving and conflict-resolution skills. Structured within the BPD course is a therapeutic framework of our relationships.

    1. Familial ties
    2. Relationship with children
    3. Work Relationships
    4. Romantic Relationships

3. *Help with regulating emotions.* Outbursts often result from frustration and not feeling heard or understood. Recognizing that you are being listened to and understood can be comforting. This workbook focuses on strategies for emotional regulation, self-reflection, relaxation, meditation, and more.

4. *Strengthen a sense of identity.* One symptom of BPD is an uncertain sense of self. When another person hears and understands your opinions or feelings, it solidifies that sense. This handbook promotes a continuity between the past, present, and future. This emphasizes the recurring idea that individuals with BPD can sometimes feel fractured and disconnected. The goal is to provide deeper insight into distorted thinking, its causes, and more effective coping strategies for dealing with feelings associated with uncertainty. Ongoing and consistent discussions about virtues, morals, goals, values, symptoms, and triggers should be prioritized. We emphasize self-acceptance, self-love, and the ability to self-soothe.

5. *Intuition.* Access to input from the body and its non-rational ways of knowing fuels wisdom. Intuition enables an understanding of one's highest good and guides one toward that goal. One's "gut sense" of things is rooted in a complex process in which the right brain makes quick and rough global assessments of one's feelings and circumstances.

6. ***Insight*** is the ability to reflect on my life experiences in a way that connects a person's past, present, and future in a coherent, cohesive, and compassionate manner. It embodies clear and accurate self-assessment and understanding and allows us to see ourselves as we truly are. Insight helps me make sense of everything that has happened in my past and what is occurring in my life now.

7. **Creating a Self-Care Plan** will help you manage your mental health. We will discuss this later in the workbook.

8. **Mindfulness Training** can help you manage your mental health. We will discuss this further later in the course.

9. *ADL/IADL:* What are the Activities of Daily Living (ADLs)? The ADLs are a series of basic activities necessary for independent living at home or in the community. They are integral to the borderline personality disorder card spread and include four basic categories: personal hygiene, dressing, and eating.

Instrumental Activities of Daily Living (IADL) are like ADLs

These actions are essential for living independently but are not necessarily required daily. Many people with borderline personality disorder and other mental health conditions struggle with them. Instrumental activities are less noticeable than activities of daily living regarding the loss of functioning.

However, the functional ability related to IADLs is typically lost before that of ADLs. Emphasizing IADLs can assist individuals with borderline personality disorder in planning, preparing, and thinking through potential issues or problems, rather than waiting until a situation leads to excessive worry or escalates to a crisis point. The IADLs are listed below.

EXERCISE 1.4: The space between the lettered items below allows you to assess and reflect on specific IADLs. Then, write a statement reflecting your assessment of your current level of functioning in each IADL area.

A. Basic communication skills - using a regular phone, mobile phone, email, or the internet.

B. Transportation - either by driving oneself, arranging rides, or the ability to use public transportation.

C. Meal preparation includes planning meals, cooking, cleaning up, storing, and safely using kitchen equipment and utensils.

D. Shopping - the ability to make appropriate food and clothing purchase decisions.

E. Housework - doing laundry, washing dishes, dusting, vacuuming, and maintaining a clean residence.

F. Managing medications - taking the correct amount at the correct time. Managing re-fills.

G. Managing personal finances - operating within a budget, writing checks, paying bills, and avoiding scams.

Managing Borderline Personality Disorder

Though we will discuss collaborative care and decision-makers, different treatment options are available if you or your loved one are diagnosed with a mental illness. Other ways to care for yourself require discipline to maintain stability. The most common mental health options include therapy and medications. There are additional activities you can pursue that involve ongoing learning and self-help. After all, your goal is improved health and quality of life.

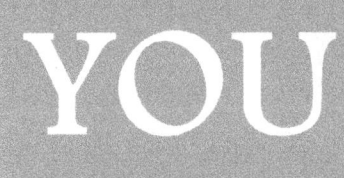

THERAPY

Psychotherapy is a common form of treatment for mental illnesses that's provided by licensed mental health professional. Therapy is a person-centered environment giving people a safe space to discuss their thoughts, feelings and behaviors to help improve quality of life

MEDICATION

Medication is not a mandatory part of mental health treatment. However, they can be prescribed by medical professionals to help aid the individual in their recovery by alleviating some of the symptoms. In extreme cases, medication might be necessary for treatment if the individual's safety is jeopardized without treatment.

PSYCHIATRIC REHABILITATION PROGRAM (PRP)

This is a mentorship program in addition to therapy that provide extra support to the individual. Mentors will collaborate with your therapist to help practice the skills learned in therapy in social settings to improve functioning. Check your insurance provider for eligibility

CASE MANAGEMENT

Individuals with an identified disability might be eligible to receive case management services through their insurance or the state. Case managers help individuals set goals that will help them work towards independence or help aid in the recovery process

GROUP THERAPY/ SUPPORT GROUPS

Group therapy or support groups are usually facilitated by mental health professionals, but with a heavy focus on group members to drive the group forward. Individuals in the group share similar experiences and provide tips and receive support on how to best to manage your illness.

INPATIENT TREATMENT

An individual's mental health symptoms may temporarily worsen. Inpatient treatment is short-term and provided in a hospital setting where symptoms can be closely monitored, medications can be adjusted to allow the person to feel well enough to return to their daily operations.

PEER SUPPORT

Peer support groups are facilitated by a trained peer specialist. They are not mental health professionals, but someone who has lived through similar experiences and is doing well in their recovery journey. Peer support groups are a helpful tool during and after completing mental health

The other treatment options illustrated in this diagram can be used simultaneously, either short-term or long-term, alongside therapy and medications to provide extra support. Important note: Verify with your insurance company which services and treatment options they cover.

> **EXERCISE 1.5:** Below are possible actions a person with borderline personality disorder can learn and enact. Each item below specifies a course of action you can implement to help you manage your illness and create long-term stability. Check those you currently enact in your life and highlight the ones you think will assist you along your healing journey.

Fear of abandonment

- ☐ Work toward building healthy relationships
- ☐ Learn about creating healthier relationships by reading books
- ☐ Spend time connecting with friends and family members for at least one hour each week
- ☐ Become involved in community activities (volunteer at an animal shelter, join a theater group
- ☐ Engage in religious services or activities
- ☐ Attend local support and self-help groups
- ☐ Identify cognitive distortions in relationships
- ☐ Learn about attachment styles and theory
- ☐ Use Dialectical Behavior skills like meditation

Unstable and Intense Relationships

- ☐ Learn about creating healthier relationships by reading books
- ☐ Practice validating others
- ☐ Practice self-validation and self-acceptance
- ☐ Commit to safety in unsafe relationships
- ☐ Be proactive in reaching out to important people
- ☐ Identify cognitive distortions in relationships

Identity Disturbance or Unstable Sense of Self

- ☐ Identify core values
- ☐ Create a list of personal and professional strengths
- ☐ Read inspiring recovery stories
- ☐ Practice self-validation and self-acceptance
- ☐ Practice self-forgiveness
- ☐ Create a personal mission statement
- ☐ Establish short-term and long-term goals

☐ Use DBT skills like accumulating positives, problem-solving, and mastery

Impulsive Behaviors

☐ Practice self-validation and self-acceptance
☐ Learn how to self-soothe
☐ Use crisis resources
☐ Create a relapse prevention and self-care plan
☐ Reach out to a sponsor, friend, or therapist before engaging in impulsive behaviors
☐ Use mindfulness and DBT distress tolerance skills (pros and cons) like DBT

Suicidal Behavior, Suicidal Threats, or Self-Harming Behaviors

☐ Practice self-validation and self-acceptance
☐ Learn how to self-soothe
☐ Make a list of reasons to stay alive
☐ Create a safety plan
☐ Use coping statements when urges to self-harm are high
☐ Use crisis resources
☐ Read *How I Stayed Alive When My Brain Was Trying to Kill Me*
☐ Use mindfulness and distress tolerance skills from DBT

Emotional Instability

☐ Practice self-validation and self-acceptance
☐ Learn how to self-soothe
☐ Reach out to support persons during a crisis
☐ Practice naming and describing emotions
☐ Journal to track and understand emotions
☐ Accept emotions instead of avoiding or pushing them away
☐ Use distress tolerance and emotion regulation skills from DBT

Emptiness or Boredom

☐ Read inspiring stories about people who have overcome obstacles
☐ Volunteer at least once a week
☐ Practice behavioral activation
☐ Engage in religious services or activities
☐ Read (or listen to) Viktor Frankl's *Man's Search for Meaning*
☐ Create art, write, or play music to alleviate boredom
☐ Use mindfulness and distress tolerance skills from DBT

Intense or Inappropriate Anger

☐ Practice self-validation and self-acceptance
☐ Learn how to self-soothe
☐ Find ways to relax and reduce stress causing anger consistently
☐ Respond with curiosity. Ask, "What is underneath the anger?"
☐ Use mindfulness, opposite action, radical acceptance, and distress tolerance skills from DBT

Paranoia or Dissociative Symptoms

☐ Practice grounding exercises
☐ Learn how to self-soothe
☐ Increase present-moment awareness
☐ Use ideas from somatic experiences to address trauma and reduce dissociative symptoms
☐ Read "Coping with Trauma-Related Dissociation"
☐ Use mindfulness, check the facts, and distress tolerance skills from DBT

General Well-Being

☐ Exercise four to six times a week for a minimum of 20 minutes
☐ Pay attention to nutrition and diet
☐ Practice sleep hygiene
☐ Refrain from using drugs or alcohol to manage emotions
☐ HALT: When emotionally dysregulated, ask yourself, "Am I **H**ungry, **H**urt, **A**ngry, **L**onely, or **T**ired?"
☐ Attend support or recovery groups
☐ Consider the role of mentors and coaches in enhancing treatment
☐ Read articles and books about BPD and related symptoms (depression, anxiety, and trauma)
☐ Keep all therapy/treatment appointments

Additional Considerations for the Therapist

☐ Help provide a framework to define mental health for the client and family members
☐ Use tools such as the Ways of Coping Checklist (see appendix) to focus on strengths
☐ Take advantage of opportunities for additional consultation and supervision
☐ Provide resources to family members
☐ Use caution when making assumptions about what the client can (or cannot) do
☐ Rule out medical causes for emotional dysregulation
☐ Assess for excessive shame within the therapeutic relationship ("I am bad for needing help.")
☐ Remain hopeful

JOURNALING

In completing this workbook, you might explore expressive art writing, including poetry, short stories, journaling, memoirs, essays, vignettes, letters, song lyrics, freewriting, reporting, speeches, blogs, video essays, and vlogs.

Are you experiencing emotional pain related to trauma, loss, grief, divorce, low self-esteem, lack of intimacy, domestic abuse, mental illness, or the loss of a loved one due to suicide? Many people struggle to process and release feelings of guilt, shame, failure, loneliness, negativity, and other intense emotions associated with these experiences. Such feelings can prevent us from reaching our full potential and thriving. Our intense experiences require expression, purging, and release.

Journaling is for everyone, not just experienced writers. All you need is interest and motivation. Come and share what's true without fear of correction, judgment, or false comfort. Acknowledging your authentic truth is liberating and heals a part of you. We encourage you to write within your comfort zone during the workshop series or as you incorporate journaling into your life.

Engaging in creative work centers you. As the author of your own story, it holds empowering significance. Your narratives resist and challenge the stories others impose on you. Perhaps you write to reinvent yourself and leave behind the old version. When you write in a journal, you gain greater control over your life and express your thoughts and feelings freely. You will also learn to shape your thoughts and intentions to gain insight and understanding.

In a later chapter, we will further explore creative self-expression.

EXERCISE 1.6: Students are encouraged to write in a journal while working through the exercises in this workbook. In your journal write about the following: What stories do people talk about you? These stories often originate in childhood. From your perspective, how do people view you? What are myths or untruths? What sort of story do you talk about yourself in the past? What future story do you want to talk about yourself?

Inspirational Quotes for People with BPD

Exercise 1.7: Below are five inspirational quotes circulating on the internet that aren't attributed to anyone. Each block provides enough space for you to respond to the quotes. 1) Rate the quotes on a scale from 1 to 10, with 10 being the highest. 2) Explain how you relate to the quotes in the space provided above or below. 3) Then, in your journal, write down five quotes you create or find elsewhere that resonate with your circumstances and that you personally appreciate.

"Even though the waves of emotion may crash over you,
You have the strength to swim back to shore.
You are not defined by your storms but by your resilience in facing them."

"Your emotions are valid, and you have the power to manage them."

"HEALING IS A JOURNEY, NOT A DESTINATION."

MODULE TWO

Improve Health-Related Quality of Life and Well-Being For All Individuals

Module Two Learning Objectives

1. Learn to maintain stability and promote your well-being by highlighting your physical, mental, and social resources.
2. Enhance the protective factors and conditions that support your health.
3. Emphasize the importance of resisting illness, building resilience, and practicing self-management.
4. Actively maintain a positive mental state and effectively manage stress, even when facing challenges.
5. Understanding that life consists of both ease and struggle, attending to necessary lifestyle changes, and practicing self-awareness and self-discipline can help individuals achieve a good quality of life and wellness.

Overview

Health-related quality of life is a multi-dimensional concept that includes domains related to physical, mental, emotional, and social functioning. It goes beyond direct measures of population health, life expectancy, and causes of death and focuses on the impact of health status on quality of life.

What is Quality of Life and Well-being?

> ***Well-being*** *refers to the beneficial aspects of a person's life, including positive emotions and satisfaction. It is a relative state that enhances physical, mental, and social functioning in supportive environments for living a full, satisfying, and productive life.*

What is Health-Related Quality of Life & Well-Being?

Healthy People 2020 emphasizes the importance of health-related quality of life and well-being, including promoting quality of life, healthy development, and health behaviors across all life stages.

The significance of quality of life and well-being has always been a human concern. The World Health Organization (WHO) states that health is "a complete physical, mental, and social well-being and not merely the absence of disease and infirmity." As people live longer than ever, researchers have shifted their focus in examining health, moving beyond just the causes of death and morbidity to exploring how health relates to the quality of an individual's life.

Quality of life in the context of health and disease is commonly referred to as health-related quality of life (HRQOL). HRQOL is multidimensional and encompasses domains related to physical, mental, emotional, and social functioning and the social context in which individuals live.

Most people work hard to *increase the quality and number of years of their healthy lives*. There are measures of life expectancy and healthy life expectancy. People want to improve their health, including their global health status, and avoid certain chronic diseases and activity limitations. For Healthy People 2020, quality of life is integral to our goals.

Promoting well-being emphasizes an individual's physical, mental, and social resources while enhancing protective factors and conditions that support health. Instead of merely viewing prevention as avoiding or minimizing illness and risk factors, well-being also highlights resisting illness, building resilience, and practicing self-management.

Healthy People 2020 Approach to Health-Related Quality of Life & Well-Being

Several existing measures of HRQOL focus on quality of life. From an integrated mental health perspective that focuses on quality of life and well-being, encompassing three complementary and related domains:

- Physical and mental health
- Overall well-being
- Participation in society

While none of these domains can fully capture the idea of health-related quality of life or well-being on their own, they offer a more effective way to assess our lives and determine our health-related quality of life and overall well-being.

Self-Rated Physical and Mental Health

HRQOL encompasses physical, mental, and social health aspects. Items have been identified as reliable and valid self-reported physical and mental health measures.

"Well-Being"

Well-being differs from individual to individual. Researchers have discovered that people generally share similar concepts regarding it. Individuals with higher levels of well-being perceive their lives as going well. They feel very healthy and energetic when participating in their daily activities. They are satisfied, interested, and engaged in their lives. They experience a sense of accomplishment in their endeavors and regard their lives as meaningful. They tend to feel more content or cheerful than depressed or anxious. They maintain good relationships with others and enjoy positive social interactions. Personal factors, social circumstances, and community environments all impact well-being.

Well-Being and Mental Illness

Well-being refers to a positive state of mental, emotional, and social health, including a sense of fulfillment, resilience, and ability to cope with life's challenges. In contrast, mental illness is a diagnosable condition that significantly affects a person's thoughts, feelings, and behaviors.

High well-being can act as a protective factor against developing mental illness, and conversely, mental illness can significantly decrease overall well-being; essentially, well-being is a broader concept that includes not just the absence of mental illness but also a *positive state of mental health*.

Key points to remember:

- **Well-being is proactive**

It involves actively taking steps to maintain a positive mental state and manage stress effectively, even when facing challenges.

- **Mental illness is a clinical condition**

It refers to a diagnosable disorder that can significantly disrupt daily functioning.

Mental Illness and feelings of satisfaction

Someone with a mental illness can still experience a high level of mental wellness if they are consistently disciplined in following through with self-care and in collaboration with mental health professionals. Also important is learning to accept and live with a mental health condition.

Individuals who have mastered their mental illness are generally more satisfied with life. A person with a mental illness tends to score lower on key well-being measures. Those with higher levels of well-being view their lives positively; they feel healthy and energetic when engaging in daily activities. They are satisfied, interested, and involved in their lives, deriving a sense of accomplishment from their activities and perceiving their lives as meaningful. Typically, they are more content or cheerful than depressed or anxious. They maintain good relationships and experience positive social interactions. Personal factors, social circumstances, and community environments influence well-being.

> *Well-being is what a person with mental illness can expect if they are diligent in attending to their self-care.*

For most people, life is a balance of ease and struggle. Achieving well-being can be challenging when emotional and mood states constantly shift, often resulting in relationship issues and other difficulties. To manage mental illness, a person needs stability. Stability comes from medications, lifestyle changes, and a significant amount of self-awareness and self-discipline to attain a good quality of life and wellness.

How is Well-being measured?

Well-being considers a person's physical, mental, and social aspects.

- **Physical well-being** relates to vigor and vitality and feeling very healthy and energetic.

- **Mental well-being** includes satisfaction with one's life, balancing positive and negative emotions, accepting oneself, finding purpose and meaning in life, seeking personal growth, autonomy, and competence, believing that one's life and circumstances are within control, and generally experiencing optimism.

- **Social well-being** involves providing and receiving support from quality family, friends, and others.

Mental well-being is often assessed through self-reported questionnaires that evaluate various aspects of positive mental health, including life satisfaction, happiness, sense of purpose, resilience, and emotional regulation. Standard scales include the Warwick-Edinburgh Mental Well-being Scale (WEMWBS), which emphasizes positive mental health and functioning.

Participation

Underlying mental health is a crucial measure of participation, indicating that a person with a functional limitation — such as vision loss, mobility difficulties, mental illness, or intellectual disability — can lead a long and productive life while enjoying a good quality of life. Poor functional status should not be equated with a poorer quality of life. Quality of life encompasses more than just activities of daily living, health statuses, disease categories, or functional abilities; it focuses on the more holistic aspects of social, psychological, and spiritual well-being. Social participation can be evaluated by assessing how individuals face barriers to full participation due to their health and environment.

Participation in society includes education, employment, and civic, social, and leisure activities, as well as participation in family roles. Participation is measured in the context of a person's current health state and social and physical environments, thus capturing a more objective construct of the HRQOL concept.

Participation, particularly social participation, is widely recognized as positively impacting mental health. Actively engaging with others in community activities can enhance mental well-being and support recovery from mental illness. Conversely, low participation is often linked to a higher risk of mental health issues such as depression and anxiety. Essentially, feeling connected to others through participation can serve as a protective factor against mental health problems.

> **EXERCISE: 2.1:** Key points about participation and mental illness (for each bullet point below, State what is a challenge for you and what is a key strength for you.)

- **Positive impact:**
  Engaging in social activities such as volunteering, joining clubs, or participating in community events can foster a sense of belonging, purpose, and self-esteem, positively affecting mental health.

- **Reduced isolation:**
  People with mental illness often experience social isolation, which can worsen symptoms. Active participation in community life can help combat this isolation and provide a support network.

- **Recovery support:**
  Participation is considered a key element in recovery-oriented mental health. It encourages individuals to participate in their well-being and re-engage with their community actively.

- **Barriers to participation:**
  Factors like the stigma associated with mental illness, lack of access to opportunities, and symptoms of the illness itself can hinder participation for individuals with mental health conditions.

> **EXERCISE 2.2:** (1) The quality-of-life quiz and test are linked below. (2) Write a synopsis of your results, and comment on whether you are surprised with your results.
>
> Quality-of-Life Scale - WHOQOL Bref Scale https://hilio.com/en/tests/quality-life-test-whoqol
>
> The Quality-of-Life Scale https://www.josephineopie.com.au/quality-of-life-quiz

ELLEN'S STORY

For as long as I can remember, my emotions felt like a wild rollercoaster, swinging from ecstatic highs to crushing lows in the blink of an eye. My emotions seemed out of control to me. I would lash out at my partner and my mom accusing them of not loving me. I constantly worried they would get tired of me and abandon me. It was like living in a constant state of emotional turbulence, where even the most minor thing could trigger a massive shift in my emotions, leaving me feeling completely out of control and often lashing out at those closest to me.

Growing up, I always felt like an outsider, struggling to maintain relationships with anyone due to my intense fear of abandonment. If someone seemed even slightly distant, I would spiral into a frenzy of suspicion and accusations, convinced they would leave me. This often-pushed people away, further reinforcing my belief that I was unlovable and unworthy. I guess I can call that self-sabotage—pushing them away so I can abandon them first so I feel more in control. That seems senseless thinking about it now.

My self-image was constantly fluctuating too; one moment I would feel confident and capable, and the next, I would be consumed by feelings of utter worthlessness. This instability is often manifested in my abuse of painkillers and even self-harm. I did these things to take away the emotional pain I experienced.

The hardest part was the internal struggle to understand my own emotions. Sometimes, I would feel empty, like a void inside me, and the only way to feel anything was to seek constant validation, go from partner to partner, and sometimes cut myself. It was a vicious cycle of intense emotions, impulsive actions, and the constant fear of being alone.

Finding a diagnosis and starting therapy was a turning point in my life. Learning about BPD helped me understand why I felt the way I did and gave me tools to manage my emotions, like mindfulness practices and cognitive behavioral therapy. While it's still a daily struggle, I've been empowered to navigate the challenges of living with BPD.

Exercise 2.3: In your journal, reflect on how you relate to Ellen's story. When did you have your "turning" point in attending to your health and wellbeing. What kind of struggles did you experience on your way to your healing journey?

MODULE THREE
Factors That Impact Your Well-Being and Life Goals

Module Three Learning Objectives

1. Learn the factors that impact your well-being and life goal
2. Understand how the bio-psycho-social-spiritual model applies to your biological, psychological, social, and spiritual dimensions to gain insight into your health and well-being.
3. Identify and address factors that affect you personally and how that can assist you in managing your symptoms.
4. Identify and define your values to understand how they influence your decisions, goals, and behavior.
5. Establish SMART goals based on your values and what is important to you.

Overview

Our program emphasizes training the mind to promote healing from mental, emotional, and physical illnesses. Grounded in the bio-psycho-social-spiritual model of care, it integrates evidence-based elements of mindfulness, cognitive-behavioral techniques, neuroscience, health psychology, positive psychology, energy psychology, and behavioral nutrition. Additionally, it highlights the healing aspects of spirituality and the influence of perception, insight, awareness, thoughts, and words, which are explored throughout this course.

The biopsychosocial-spiritual model (BPSS) is a framework that considers a person's biological, psychological, social, and spiritual dimensions to understand their health and well-being. The model is based on the idea that health and illness result from the interaction between these factors.

What is the Whole Self Wellbeing Model

- A comprehensive model that considers all aspects of a person's health
- A model that recognizes that people are complex beings
- A model that considers how changes in one aspect can affect other aspects

How it's used

- Used in social work and mental health to assess a person's health
- Used to understand how addiction is caused by a complex interplay of factors
- Used to understand how physical, psychological, and social factors contribute to medical conditions

The BPSS model builds on the biopsychosocial model initially developed by George L. Engel in 1977. This model was designed to address the limitations of the biomedical approach, which only considered biological aspects of illness. The BPSS model emerged in response to the World Health Assembly's recommendation to include the spiritual dimension in health care.

FOUR DOMAINS TO WHOLE SELF WELL-BEING MODEL

Practitioners and others who aim to consider the whole person instead of just a label or diagnosis can utilize the BPSS model. This model can also serve in medical and mental health education to address physical, psychological, social, and spiritual needs.

Some ways to incorporate spirituality into the BPSS model include (Saad 2017):

- Journaling or reflective writing about spiritual experiences and growth
- Spiritual counseling or guidance from chaplains or spiritual leaders
- Spending time in nature or doing outdoor activities

In the bio-psycho-social-spiritual model, "spirituality" refers to an individual's connection to something greater than themselves. It includes their search for meaning, purpose, and values in life, often expressed through beliefs, practices, and experiences related to religion, nature, or a higher power. Spirituality can significantly influence an individual's overall well-being and health.

Key points about spirituality in the biopsychosocial model:

- **Beyond religion:**
  While spirituality can be intertwined with religious beliefs, it is not limited to organized religion. It can include personal connections to nature, a sense of inner peace, or a belief in a higher purpose.

- **Impact on health:**
  Considering a person's spiritual dimension within the biopsychosocial model can provide a holistic understanding of their health and well-being, as their spiritual beliefs can influence their coping mechanisms, resilience, and outlook on life.

- **Areas of exploration:**
  When assessing someone's spirituality within this model, we may explore values, meaning-making practices, rituals, beliefs about life and death, and our sense of connection to a larger community.

Bio-psycho-social-spiritual Model: Factors that impact your life goals

Gaining insight into your BPD and mental health life goals can help you identify what makes your symptoms better or worse. Understanding the factors that affect you personally can assist you in managing your symptoms – first, by helping you recognize them, and second, by promoting healthy responses that move you closer to your life goals.

This chapter focuses on understanding the BPSS model and the factors influencing mental health. We will take some time to review the lists related to the model's factors that are specific to you.

Many more specific factors can affect life goals, including:

- **Education**: Accurate health, nutrition, and exercise information can help you make informed decisions.

- **Fear of failure**: Fear of failure can prevent people from acting towards their goals.

- **Personal development**: Believing that your goals are attainable can improve well-being.

- **Positive attitude**: A positive attitude can help you deal with stress and be grateful for the good things in life.

- **Life satisfaction**: Setting and achieving essential goals can enhance your well-being and life satisfaction.

- **Self-esteem:** Working towards goals can help you develop an ideal self-image.
- **Obstacles:** Putting off goals, waiting to act, and not anticipating challenges can make it harder to achieve them.

PSYCHO-SOCIAL-BIOLOGICAL-SPIRITUAL MODEL

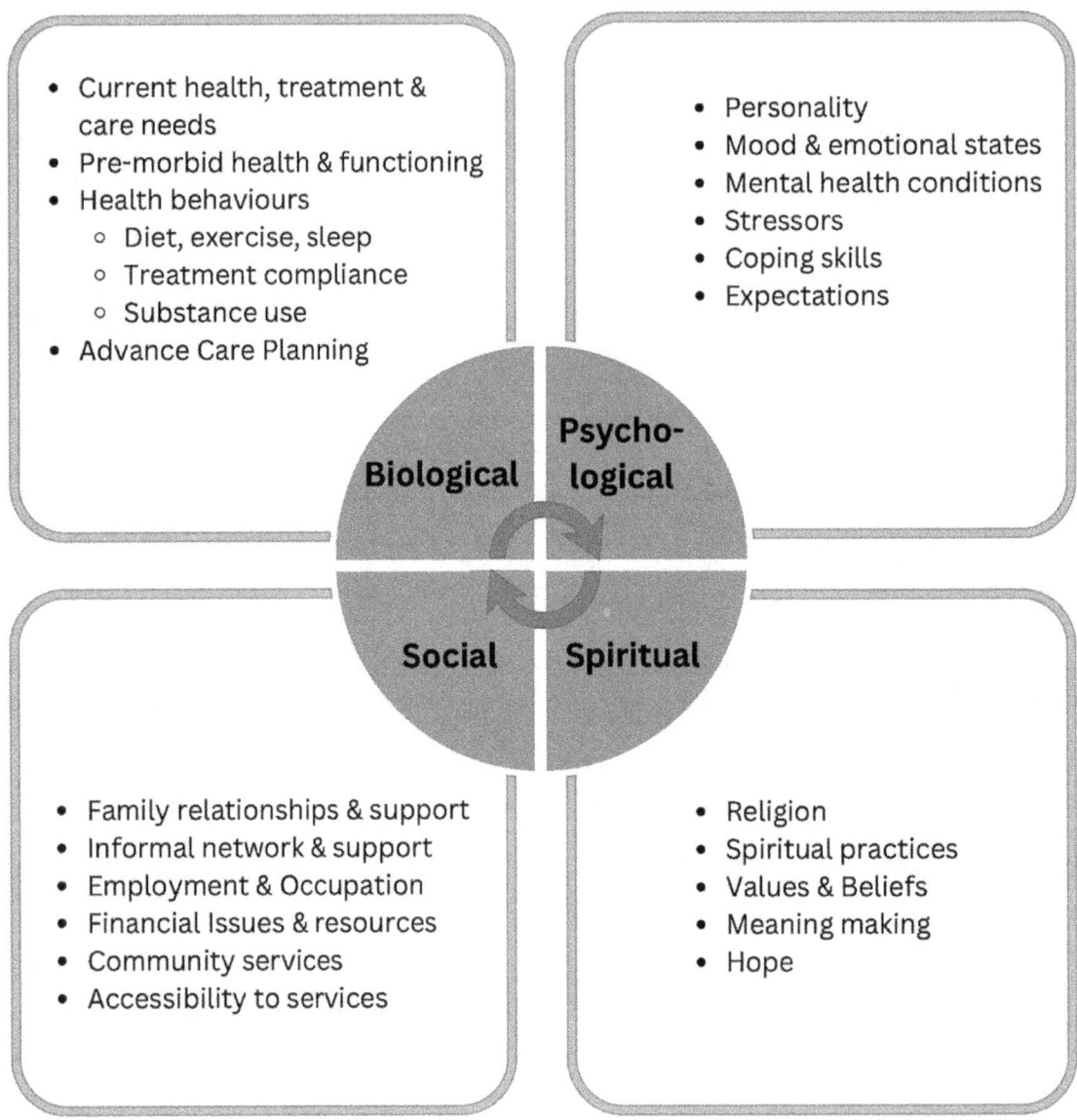

Biological factors include poor sleep, substance use or abuse, heredity, medical issues, poor nutrition, pain management, and exercise, among others.

- Current health, treatment & care needs
- Pre-morbid health & functioning
- Health behaviors
  - Diet, exercise, sleep
  - Treatment compliance
  - Substance use
- Advance Care Planning

Psychological factors include difficulty concentrating, traumatic events, the death of a loved one, a challenging childhood, pain management, and other personal experiences.

- Personality
- Mood & emotional states
- Mental health conditions
- Stressors
- Coping skills
- Expectations

Social factors – financial concerns, isolation, social support, and others.

- Family relationships & support
- Informal network & support
- Employment & Occupation
- Financial Issues & resources
- Community services
- Accessibility to services

> Your value doesn't decrease based on someone's inability to see your worth

> **Exercise 3.1: The "I Am" Poem.** This activity begins an active introspective process while continuing to provide opportunities for individuals to make connections with each other. Participants write short poems, starting each line with "I am," encouraging them to describe in their own words who they are and what's salient to their identities.

"Who Am I" poems are a way for people to express their thoughts about who they are and where they come from. The instructions for writing a "Who Am I" poem include:

- **Brainstorm**: Consider what makes you who you are, such as your interests, family, memories, or beliefs. Ask a friend, family member, or child to write their poem so you can share.

- **Write**: Start each line with the words "I am" and write about your thoughts

Here are some tips for writing a "Who Am I" poem:

- **Be open**: Let your poem be open to your interpretation

- **Be descriptive**: Use descriptive language to build a world around your first line

- **Be vulnerable**: Share your poem first to make others feel more comfortable sharing theirs

- **Be creative**: Include vivid memories, exaggerations, or dialogue

I AM POEM TEMPLATE

I am _____ (Two unique characteristics)

I wonder _____ (Something you are curious about)

I hear _____ (An imaginary sound)

I see _____ (An imaginary sight)

I want _____ (A desire you have)

I am _____ (The first line of the poem repeated)

I pretend _____ (Something you pretend to do)

I feel _____ (A feeling about something imaginary)

I touch _____ (An imaginary touch)

I worry _____ (Something that bothers you)

I cry _____ (Something that makes you sad)

I am _____ (The first line of the poem repeated)

I understand _____ (Something you know is true)

I say _____ (Something you believe in)

I dream _____ (Something you dream about)

I try _____ (Something you try on)

I hope _____ (Something you hope for)

I am _____ (The first line of the poem repeated)

WORKING FROM YOUR CORE VALUES

Values are principles that guide one's actions in every aspect of life. They represent the reasons behind our chosen goals (the "whys" in life). In other words, values reflect what we believe and what is important to us.

Values are what you believe in. They:

- Make life worth living
- Make you a unique human being
- Define who you are
- Give you a sense of "self"

We usually know our values, but how often do we name them and let them inspire us to act?

What is a Value?

1. Qualities, characteristics, or ideas about which you feel strongly.

2. Our values affect our decisions, goals, and behavior.

3. A belief or feeling that someone or something is worthwhile.

4. Values define what is of worth, what is beneficial, and what is harmful to us.

5. Values are standards to guide your actions, judgments, and decisions

PERSONAL VALUES

DEFINITION

Personal values are deeply held beliefs and principles that guide individuals in their thoughts, actions, and decision-making. They reflect what is important to a person and shape their identity and behavior. Personal values are often influenced by factors such as culture, family, religion, mentors, and personal experiences.

EXAMPLES

- **Loyalty** - This value emphasizes unwavering commitment, trust, and support towards friends, family, and other in-groups.

- **Fairness** - This value emphasizes treating others equitably and upholding impartiality, ensuring that everyone is given equal opportunities and fair treatment.

A SENSE OF WHO YOU ARE

A "value" is a deeply held belief or principle that guides our actions and decisions, representing what we consider essential in life. It's crucial for our life goals because it acts as a compass, ensuring our goals align with our core beliefs, leading to a more fulfilling and meaningful path. A typical example of a value is "Family first." This value might guide someone to set goals like spending quality time with loved ones or prioritizing family events when making plans.

> **EXERCISE 3.2** Key points about values and life goals are below. In the space provided, answer the question reflects questions related to the value category.

- **What are a few of your guiding principles?**
  Values act as a framework for decision-making, helping us choose paths that resonate with our priorities.

- **What is your motivation and purpose?**
  Goals rooted in our values provide a strong sense of purpose and intrinsic motivation to achieve them.

- **Authenticity: Do your goals and values align with who you are?**
  Aligning your goals with your values ensures you pursue what truly matters to you, leading to a more authentic life.

- **Decision-making clarity:** Do you understand your values that can help you make better decisions and stay on track toward your goals? List a few below.

- **Emotional well-being:** Achieving goals that align with your values can foster a sense of accomplishment and personal fulfillment, contributing to your happiness. Write a few sentences reflecting on your current emotional wellness.

Values inform our decisions and actions

Values are the compass that guides our lives, helping us make decisions that align with our aspired selves. Understanding and defining our core values is essential for leading an intentional and fulfilling life. By embracing important values that resonate with us, we can navigate life's challenges with integrity and consistency, ensuring we stay true to ourselves. Committing to these values allows us to create a life that is not only successful but also meaningful and authentic.

Values are forward-learning

Valuegraphics discovered in a survey of 500,000 people across 152 languages regarding what individuals perceive as shared values. Among the responses on the list of shared values are freedom of speech, leisure, and financial security.

What we care about changes daily—every minute, even—and it's hard to agree on a list of values. When your kid is having a tantrum, you care about finding some peace and quiet. When you're stuck in bumper-to-bumper traffic with an empty fuel tank, you care about whether there's a gas station nearby. However, these situations do not represent values.

Understanding and defining your core values is essential because values are more forward-thinking than reactions to immediate situations. Values shape our decisions and behaviors, guiding us toward the person we aspire to be. They help us make choices that align with our true selves, fostering integrity and personal growth.

When we define values as attributes of the people we aspire to be, our next steps become clearer. My wife and I "care about" our daughter, but that's not actionable. What's actionable is our desire to be attentive parents. Attentiveness is a value. If we both want to be attentive parents, we can discuss what that means and strive each day to embody it. It means being fully present together without getting distracted by our phones.

EXERCISE 3.3. Add two or three personal values and discuss how it relates to your future and application in your daily life:

1.

2.

3.

WHAT DO WE CARE ABOUT MOST

A list of things people generally care about the most could include family and loved ones, health and well-being, personal growth, financial security, meaningful work, social connection, personal values, contributing to the community, environmental sustainability, and overall happiness; the specific priorities can vary depending on individual life stages and circumstances.

Most people tend to care most about their close relationships with family and friends, often prioritizing love, connection, and the well-being of those closest to them; this includes spouses, children, parents, and close friends, as these relationships are considered foundational to happiness and a sense of belonging. Often, people who have mental illnesses experience relationship challenges more so than most. Sometimes, they may feel alienated, like they don't "belong."

Key points about what people typically care about most:

- **Strong social connections:**
  Feeling loved and supported by a close network is generally considered the most critical factor in most people's lives.

- **Personal health and well-being:**
  Maintaining physical and mental health is a significant concern for many individuals.

- **Meaningful work or purpose:**
  A job or activity that provides a sense of accomplishment and contributes to a greater good can be highly motivating.

- **Financial security:**
  Ensuring that basic needs like food and shelter are met is a priority for most people.

- **Personal growth and development:**
  Many individuals value learning new skills, expanding their knowledge, and striving to become better versions of themselves.

Here's a more detailed breakdown of potential categories:

- **Personal:**
    - Health and fitness
    - Mental well-being
    - Personal growth and development
    - Self-esteem and confidence
    - Quality of life

- **Relationships:**
    - Family and friends
    - Romantic relationships
    - Belonging and connection
    - Intimacy and trust

- **Career and Life Purpose:**

    - Meaningful work
    - Career advancement and satisfaction
    - Financial stability
    - Work-life balance

- **Social and Civic:**
    - Community involvement
    - Social justice issues
    - Environmental protection
    - Making a positive impact

- **Personal Values:**
    - Honesty and integrity
    - Compassion and empathy
    - Fairness and equality
    - Respect for others
    - Personal freedom

Until you value yourself, you won't value your time. Until you value your time, you will not do anything with it.

***

M. SCOTT PECK

EXERCISE 3.4: Core Values Exercise

Determine your core values. From the list below, choose every core value that resonates with you. Do not overthink your selection. As you read through the list, write down the words that feel like core values. If you think of a value you possess that is not on the list, write it down.

LIST OF CORE VALUES

_ Abundance	_ Dedication	_ Kindness	_ Professionalism
_ Acceptance	_ Dependability	_ Knowledge	_ Punctuality
_ Accountability	_ Diversity	_ Leadership	_ Relationships
_ Achievement	_ Empathy	_ Learning	_ Reliability
_ Adventure	_ Encouragement	_ Love	_ Resilience
_ Advocacy	_ Enthusiasm	_ Loyalty	_ Resourcefulness
_ Ambition	_ Ethics	_ Making a Difference	_ Responsibility
_ Appreciation	_ Excellence	_ Mindfulness	_ Responsiveness
_ Attractiveness	_ Expressiveness	_ Motivation	_ Security
_ Autonomy	_ Fairness	_ Optimism	_ Self-Control
_ Balance	_ Family	_ Open-Mindedness	_ Selflessness
_ Being the Best	_ Friendships	_ Originality	_ Simplicity
_ Benevolence	_ Flexibility	_ Passion	_ Stability
_ Boldness	_ Freedom	_ Performance	_ Success
_ Brilliance	_ Fun	_ Personal Development	_ Teamwork
_ Calmness	_ Generosity	_ Proactive	_ Thankfulness
_ Caring	_ Grace	_ Professionalism	_ Thoughtfulness
_ Challenge	_ Growth	_ Quality	_ Traditionalism
_ Charity	_ Flexibility	_ Recognition	_ Trustworthiness
_ Cheerfulness	_ Happiness	_ Risk Taking	_ Understanding
_ Cleverness	_ Health	_ Safety	_ Uniqueness
_ Community	_ Honesty	_ Security	_ Usefulness
_ Commitment	_ Humility	_ Service	_ Versatility
_ Compassion	_ Humor	_ Spirituality	_ Vision
_ Cooperation	_ Inclusiveness	_ Stability	_ Warmth
_ Collaboration	_ Independence	_ Peace	_ Wealth
_ Consistency	_ Individuality	_ Perfection	_ Well-Being
_ Contribution	_ Innovation	_ Playfulness	_ Wisdom
_ Creativity	_ Inspiration		_ Zeal
_ Credibility	_ Intelligence		
_ Curiosity	_ Intuition		

EXERCISE 3.5: In the space below, identify and express your values. You can read ahead if you wish to get help with your answer.

1. Give an example of something (big or small) you have done in the last week that demonstrates one of your values.

2. Which values have you identified today that can help "inspire you to action" to manage your health better?

EXERCISE 3.6 Identifying Your Life Goals

A goal is something that you want to have or achieve in your life. Goals are often related to our values – for example, if one of your values is being a good parent, a goal might be to improve your relationship with your children.

What are some life goals that you have for your life? For your health? What areas would you like to work on in terms of managing your health and getting more out of your life? Let's focus on what's important to you.

1. The Life Goals that are important to me:

2. The Life Goal I want to focus on today:

3. The value(s) that drives me toward this goal:

Set SMART goals:

- **Specific:** Clearly define what you want to achieve, including details like "where," "when," and "how."

- **Measurable:** Establish a way to track your progress with concrete metrics

- **Attainable:** Ensure your goal is realistic and achievable based on your current situation

- **Relevant:** Make sure your goal aligns with your values and overall life direction

- **Time-bound:** Set a deadline for achieving your goal

Break down significant goals:

- **Create milestones:** Divide your big goal into smaller, manageable steps

- **Action plan:** Outline specific actions you need to take to reach each milestone

Write down or make visual your goals:

- **Create a vision board:** Vision boards can help you clarify your goals, stay focused, and feel more motivated. They can also help you develop a positive mindset and improve your creativity.

- **Journaling:** Regularly write down your goals to solidify them in your mind

- **Visualize success and act upon it:** Imagine yourself achieving your goals and how it would feel

Act and track progress:

- **Regular review:** Check in with yourself periodically to assess your progress and adjust your plan if needed

- **Celebrate achievements:** Acknowledge and reward yourself for reaching milestones

---

EXERCISE 3.7—Write down your personal goals. First, reflect on what you want to achieve to set life goals. Then, use the SMART framework to create specific, measurable, attainable, relevant, and time-bound goals. Write them down, break them into smaller actionable steps, and regularly track your progress to stay motivated and on track to achieving them. In your journal, using the **SMART** format, list two shorter-term goals you want to accomplish in the next 1-3 years. Then, list two three-to-five-year goals.

LIFELINE TO IMMEDIATE HELP!

<u>Suicide Prevention Lifeline</u>
988

<u>Warm Lines</u>
These are peer-run organizations and may not be available 24/7.

<u>Crisis Text Line</u>
If you can't talk, text.

<u>Samaritans NYC</u>
1-212-673-3000

<u>Veterans Crisis Line</u>
1-800-273-8255 (Press 1) or text 838255

<u>RAINN</u>
Sexual assault hotline
1-800-656-4673

<u>National Alliance on Mental Illness (NAMI) Crisis Text Line</u>
Text 741741
Again, if you can't talk, text.

MODULE FOUR

Symptoms, Triggers, and Proactive Planning

Module Four Learning Objectives

1. Identify the symptoms that may differ and affect your overall quality of life and the achievement of your life goals.
2. Learn about the relationship between symptoms and how they are triggered by the choices you make within the context of the bio-socio-psycho-spiritual model.
3. Determine what interventions can help you alleviate the severity and consequences of your symptoms.
4. Identify your triggers, understand how they connect to your mental health symptoms, and create a proactive plan to lessen their negative impacts on your mental well-being.
5. Create and recognize your unhealthy reactions to potential triggers and deliberately think about a more suitable or healthier response.

Overview

Living with borderline personality disorder can be complex. As you know, while the severity of BPD varies, coping with it often presents challenges. Although there is no cure, many symptoms can be alleviated and may even go into remission at times. Within the bio-socio-psycho-spiritual model, we observe how one area of life can influence others. This module examines what we can control and what is beyond our control. Your symptoms may differ and affect your overall quality of life and the achievement of your life goals. Symptoms can sometimes be triggered by our choices within the bio-socio-psycho-spiritual model, which could help prevent symptoms from arising.

Identifying Symptoms and Triggers

Here are some questions we will ask and you will answer in this chapter:

1) What symptoms are you experiencing?
2) How long have you been experiencing these symptoms?
3) How frequently do you encounter symptoms?
4) How would you rate the severity of your symptoms and their impact on your quality of life?
5) In what ways are your symptoms affecting your daily life?
6) Is there anything that triggers your symptoms or makes them worse?
7) Are there any early warning signs that precede the onset of your symptoms?
8) What interventions can help alleviate the severity and consequences of your symptoms?

Relationship between BPD symptoms and DSM Diagnostic Criteria

Because BPD is a particularly severe form of personality disorder, those affected often make up a relatively large percentage of patients receiving mental health treatment. It impacts 1% to 2% of American adults, approximately 10% of psychiatric outpatients, and 15% to 20% of psychiatric inpatients. An astonishing 69% to 80% of patients with BPD exhibit suicidal behavior (including suicide attempts and life-threatening actions), and up to 9% of patients with BPD die by suicide (Linehan et al., 2015).

According to research on borderline personality disorder and the creator of Dialectical Behavior Therapy (DBT), childhood adversity and *abuse—especially sexual abuse—have long been considered significant risk factors* for developing BPD. Some studies indicate that 81% to 91% of BPD patients experienced abuse during childhood. However, other researchers argue that risk does not equate to causation and that recall bias may have influenced earlier studies, particularly when patients were questioned years later.

The prevailing view on BPD now suggests that it arises from the interaction of multiple factors, such as trauma in children who are temperamentally or genetically predisposed. Indeed, family and twin studies indicate that BPD is 69% heritable, meaning that genetics account for much of the susceptibility to develop this disorder (Linehan et al., 2015).

Diagnostic criteria of borderline personality disorder

The *Diagnostic and Statistical Manual of Mental Disorders, Fifth Edition*, defines borderline personality disorder as a pervasive pattern of instability of interpersonal relationships, self-image and affects, and marked impulsivity beginning by early adulthood and present in a variety of contexts, as indicated by 5 (or more) of the following (mark those that apply to you):

1. Frantic efforts to avoid real or imagined abandonment. Note: Do not include suicidal or self-mutilating behavior covered in criterion 5.

2. A pattern of unstable and intense interpersonal relationships characterized by alternating between extremes of idealization and devaluation.

3. Identity disturbance: markedly and persistently unstable self-image or sense of self.

4. Impulsivity in at least 2 areas that are potentially self-damaging (e.g., spending, sex, substance abuse, reckless driving, binge eating). Note: Do not include suicidal or self-mutilating behavior covered in criterion 5.

5. Recurrent suicidal behavior, gestures, or threats, or self-mutilating behavior.

6. Affective instability due to a marked reactivity of mood (e.g., intense episodic dysphoria, irritability, or anxiety, usually lasting a few hours and only rarely more than a few days).

7. Chronic feelings of emptiness.

8. Inappropriate, intense anger or difficulty controlling anger (e.g., frequent displays of temper, constant anger, recurrent physical fights).

9. Transient, stress-related paranoid ideation or severe dissociative symptoms.

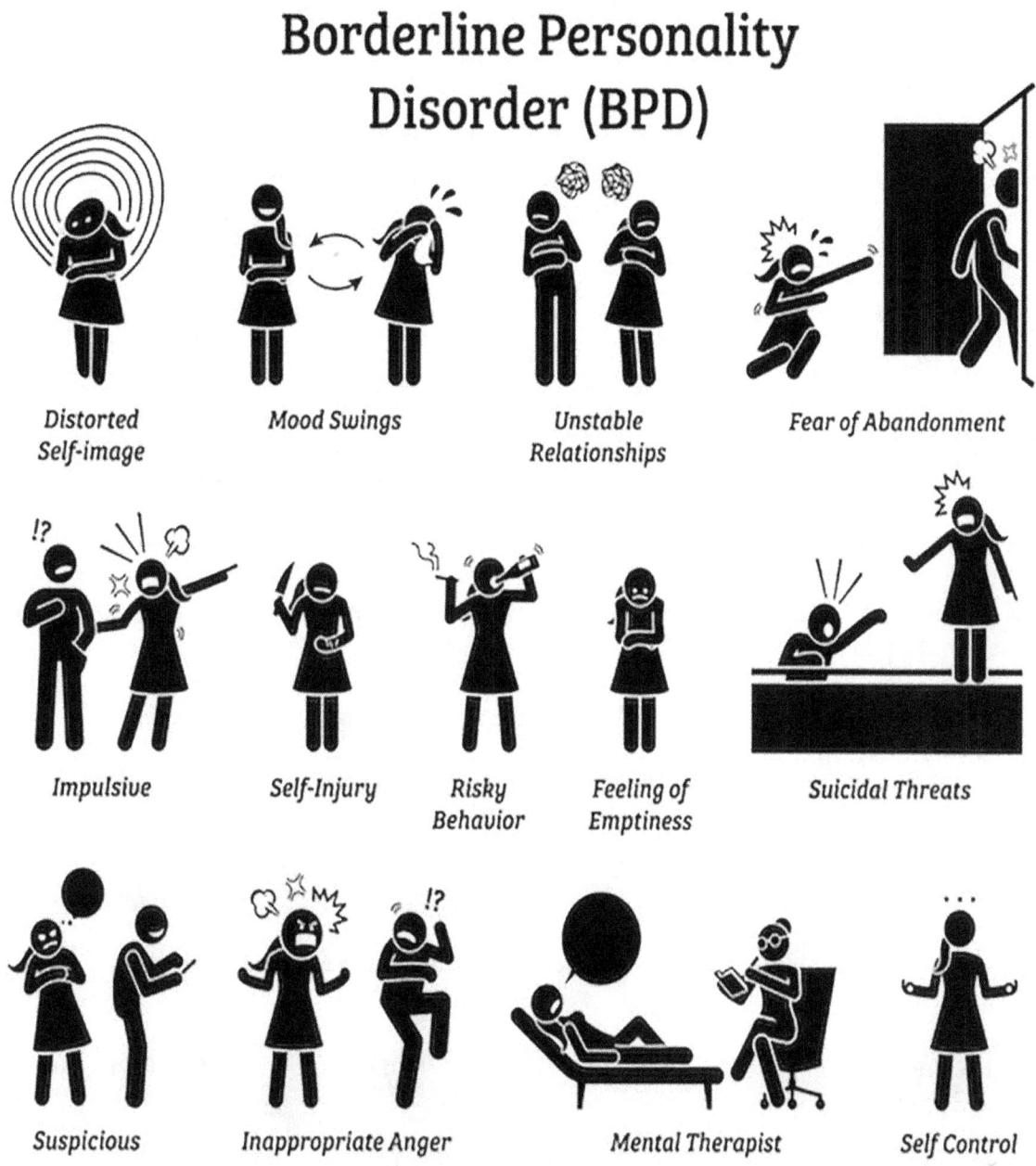

ASSESSMENT OF LIVING SKILLS INVENTORY ADL/IADL:

A very important aspect of managing any mental illness is Activities of Daily Living (ADLs). The Activities of Daily Living (IADL) are a series of basic activities necessary for independent living at home or in the community that are integral to the functioning of the person with borderline personality disorder. On a Maslow pyramid, this represents the base or bottom quadrant. If a person with mental illness can't master this area of functioning, they will likely be dependent on others for their existence. Life areas include eleven basic task categories, including personal hygiene, dressing, eating, etc.

Many people with borderline personality and other disorders struggle with them. Instrumental activities are not as noticeable as activities of daily living in terms of loss of functioning. However, functional ability for

IADLs is generally lost before ADLs. Emphasis on IADLs can help a person to plan, prepare, and think through potential issues or problems rather than waiting until the situation causes excessive worry or develops to a crisis point (Camp & Hubley, 1998).

What are the Activities of Daily Living (ADLs)? The ADLs are basic tasks essential for independent living at home or in the community. They are crucial for the functioning of individuals with borderline personality disorder and include 11 fundamental categories, such as personal hygiene, dressing, eating, and several others.

On a Maslow pyramid, this represents the base or bottom quadrant. If a person with mental illness can't master this area of functioning, they will likely be dependent on others for their existence. Life areas include eleven basic task categories, including personal hygiene, dressing, eating, etc.

Emphasis on IADLs can help a person plan, prepare, and think through potential issues or problems rather than wait until the situation causes excessive worry or develops to a crisis point (Camp & Hubley, 1998).

Activities of daily living examples

Here's a standard list of activities of daily living, as outlined by the Katz Index of Independence in Activities of Daily Living:

- Bathing and showering — the ability to bathe and maintain personal hygiene.

- Continence — complete control of the bowels and bladder.

- Dressing — choosing suitable clothing and outerwear for the weather or occasion and getting dressed independently.

- Mobility — the ability to walk or transfer from one place to another, particularly in and out of a bed or chair

- Feeding (excluding meal preparation) — the ability to move food from the plate to the mouth and to chew and swallow

- Toileting — the ability to get on and off the toilet and clean oneself without assistance

ADLs are essential human functions. How can we care for ourselves and the level of help and support a person needs? Most of us can functionally perform ADLs with exceptions.

INSTRUMENTAL ACTIVITIES OF DAILY LIVING (IADLS)

Focusing on IADLs can assist individuals diagnosed with BPD in planning, preparing, and considering potential issues or challenges instead of waiting for the situation to lead to excessive worry or reach a crisis point (Camp & Hubley, 1998).

Why are IADLs important?

- IADLs can significantly improve quality of life

- IADLs are essential for independent living in the community

The IADL areas applicable to everyone but specifically emphasized for individuals with BPD are as follows.

- **Strengthening relationships.** Relationships are all about understanding and sharing. As one of the symptoms of BPD is a history of stormy relationships, it's no wonder that finding the support of someone who can validate what you are saying can be a step in the direction of healing.

- **Helping with emotion regulation.** Outbursts often stem from frustration. Frustration often stems from not being listened to or understood. Realizing you are being listened to and understood is soothing.

- **Strengthening a sense of identity.** One of the symptoms of BPD is an uncertain sense of identity. Having another person hear and understand your opinion or feelings on a matter solidifies the foundation of who you are

> **EXERCISE 4.1:** For each bullet point below, rate your performance on each IADL using a scale from 1 to 10, where 10 indicates the highest effectiveness. Include a comment that suggests actions you can take to enhance your score in this skill area.

√ **Managing finances**: Paying bills, managing financial assets

√ **Managing transportation**: Driving, organizing other transportation

√ **Shopping**: Buying groceries, clothing, and other items

√ **Meal preparation**: Cooking and preparing meals

√ **Housekeeping**: Cleaning and maintaining the home

√ **Managing medications**: Obtaining medications and taking them as directed

√ **Managing communication:** Using the phone, mail, or other communication devices

√ **Running errands:** Shopping, picking up prescriptions, or running other errands

√ **Taking care of pets:** Caring for pets

√ **Maintaining the property:** Keeping up with home maintenance

√ **Engaging in hobbies:** Participating in hobbies

MENTAL HEALTH SYMPTOMS AND TRIGGERS

> *Mental health triggers* are stimuli that can cause or worsen mental health symptoms. They can cause intense emotional or psychological reactions, such as fear, panic, or flashbacks.

Common triggers for someone with borderline personality disorder (BPD) include perceived or real abandonment, rejection of any kind, criticism, relationship conflicts, loss of a job, stressful life events, reminders of past trauma, changes in routine, feelings of loneliness, and situations that evoke negative memories, all of which can trigger intense emotional responses due to the heightened sensitivity to feelings of insecurity and fear of being alone.

Nine Common BPD Triggers

The End of a Relationship	Feeling Ignored	Being Talked About
Being in a Crowded Place	Being Criticized	Last Minute Changes in Plans
Changes in Routine	Rejection or Feeling Abandoned	Reminders of Traumatic Events

Separations, disagreements, and rejections—real or perceived—are the most common triggers for symptoms. A person with BPD is highly sensitive to abandonment and being alone, which brings about intense feelings of anger, fear, suicidal thoughts, self-harm, and very impulsive decisions.

How triggers relate to mental health symptoms:

- **Physical reactions:**
  Triggers can cause physical responses, such as sweating, heavy breathing, or crying.

- **Emotional reactions:**
  Triggers can cause emotional reactions, such as feeling overwhelmed, scared, or powerless.

- **Behavior:**
  Triggers can cause behaviors that range from minor, like crying, to severe, like violence.

- **Judgment**
  Triggers can impair judgment and awareness.

> **EXERCISE 4.2:** Triggers vary significantly from one individual to another. Various stimuli can serve as potential triggers, often profoundly shaped by past experiences. For each of the listed triggers below, identify and note what specific triggers you experience. Add a second statement on how you cope with each.

- **External triggers:** Consider the senses—sounds, sights, smells, and textures that evoke responses shaped by past experiences. For example, the scent of the cologne worn by a loved one who has passed away can evoke feelings of grief.

- **Internal triggers: Intense emotions that stem from previous experiences.** For example, making a doctor's appointment following an adverse medical experience can evoke fear.

- **Trauma triggers:** Linked to intense feelings that arise from past trauma. For instance, the sound of firecrackers can evoke trauma in war veterans.

- **Symptom triggers:** A physical change can lead to more serious mental health issues. For instance, insufficient sleep might trigger symptoms of borderline personality disorder.

UNDERSTANDING AND IDENTIFYING TRIGGERS CAN BE EMPOWERING

Consequences of triggers:

- A trigger might cause a physical response – heavy breathing, sweating, crying.
- A trigger can elicit an emotional reaction, like thinking, "I am being attacked."
- A trigger can cause harm or a relapse.

After experiencing a trigger, a person may have strong negative feelings, such as feelings of being overwhelmed, powerless, and fearful. These emotions can be harmful to mental health and are often challenging to address effectively once they arise.

The behavior that arises after a trigger can vary from relatively mild (crying) to severe (acts of violence). A person exposed to a trigger may experience diminished judgment or awareness.

Ways to Respond to Triggers

√ Take a step back and recognize the source of your intense feelings.

√ Remind yourself that you are safe.

√ Practice slow, deep breathing.

√ Repeat a mantra in your mind.

√ Use Cognitive or Dialectical Behavior Techniques

√ Release your feelings through artistic creation.

> **EXERCISE 4.3:** Below is a list of potential trigger reactions you may experience. As you read below, checkmark those that apply to you, add any others, and make a statement about them.

- **Physical reactions:** Heavy breathing, sweating, crying, headaches, body pains, stomach problems, and skin rashes

- **Emotional reactions:** Fear, anger, sadness, worry, numbness, frustration, overwhelm, powerlessness, negative self-talk, self-sabotage, outbursts, and self-injurious behaviors

- **Behavioral reactions:** Crying, pacing, being argumentative, or acts of violence

- **Cognitive reactions:** Difficulty concentrating and making decisions, impaired judgment, or negative patterns of thinking

- **Sleep problems:** Difficulty sleeping or nightmares, or a cycle of worrying and sleeplessness

- **Appetite changes:** Loss of appetite or binge eating

- **Substance use:** Increased use of tobacco, alcohol, and other substances

- **Worsening of chronic health problems:** Worsening of mental health conditions

TRIGGERS, STRESS, AND RESPONSES

> *Triggers are external events, situations, or circumstances that can cause significant emotional or psychological discomfort. They vary significantly from one individual to another.*

Identifying Symptoms and Triggers

Living with a borderline personality disorder can be complicated. As you know, while the severity of BPD varies, living with it can often be a challenge. Although there is no cure, many symptoms can be treated, and sometimes, they go into remission. Within the bio/socio/psycho/spiritual model, we can see how one area may affect other areas of our life. There are things we can control and others we cannot. As you recognize, your symptoms may vary and affect your overall quality of life and achievement of life goals. Symptoms are sometimes triggered by the decisions we make within the context of the bio-socio-psych-spiritual model that may prevent symptoms from occurring.

What can you do about triggers?

- Recognize and address triggers appropriately
- Develop plans to avoid or deal with triggering events
- Seek out social connections to prevent isolation and loneliness

Symptoms and Responses

EXERCISE 4.4: Check off each symptom you experience by placing a mark to the Left. Use the blank lines to add any symptoms not already listed. Then, indicate how long you have had each symptom and how frequently you experience it, rate its impact on your quality of life, identify potential triggers, note early warning signs before symptoms begin, and list any interventions that help reduce the severity of your symptoms.

1) Abandonment anxieties
   a) *State how you are affected and respond:*

2) Unstable relationships/splitting
   a) *State how you are affected and respond:*

3) Identity Disturbance
    a) *State how you are affected and respond:*

4) Impulsivity/Reckless/Obsession/Addictions
    a) *State how you are affected and respond:*

5) Suicidal Behavior/Self-Harm
    a) *State how you are affected and respond:*

6) Feelings/Mood Swings/Affect/Depression
    a) *State how you are affected and respond:*

7) Feelings Of Emptiness
    a) *State how you are affected and respond:*

8) Angry/Hostile/Bitter/Revengeful/Mean-Spirited
    a) *State how you are affected and respond:*

9) Paranoid And Dissociating
    a) *State how you are affected and respond:*

10) Bad life events
    a) *State how you are affected and respond:*

11) Good Life events
    a) State how you are affected and respond:

12) Medication changes
    a) State how you are affected and respond:

13) Problems with physical health
    a) State how you are affected and respond:

14) Drug or alcohol use
    a) State how you are affected and respond:

15) Change in Seasons
    a) State how you are affected and respond:

16) Change in Routines
    a) State how you are affected and respond:

17) Problems with person of interest
    a) State how you are affected and respond:

18) Problems with children/family members
    a) State how you are affected and respond:

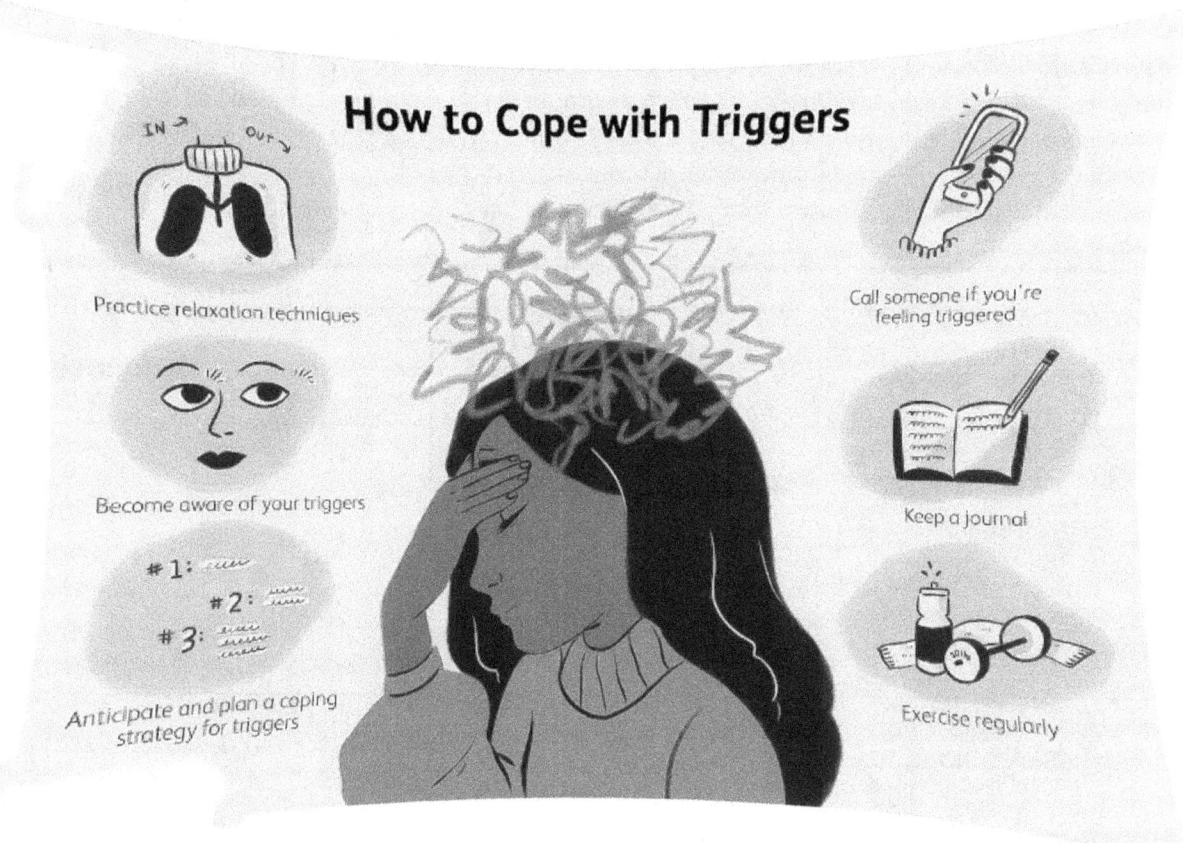

TRIGGER/RESPONSE GRID

A *healthy response* is a way of reacting to a respectful, empathetic situation, which benefits those involved. It can also refer to coping with stress or past traumatic experiences. A healthy response reflects your best interests and minimizes harm.

Experts suggest that emotionally healthy individuals experience fewer negative emotions and quickly recover from challenges. This ability is known as resilience. Developing effective coping strategies and utilizing community resources can help enhance your resilience.

A mental health trigger is a stimulus that provokes a reaction, often leading to a negative emotional response that worsens the symptoms of a mental illness. Triggers can be either physical or emotional and may originate from various sources.

Individuals who have experienced trauma or are recovering from mental health challenges, including self-harm, addiction, and eating disorders, may face unresolved triggers. For those with a history of these issues, unexpected exposure to images or content related to their past can be damaging.

Various stimuli can serve as potential triggers, often heavily shaped by past experiences.

Understanding, identifying, and working to *prevent* triggers can be both empowering and effective, particularly when compared to supporting someone after they have been triggered.

EXERCISE 4.5: Below are common triggers you may have encountered. This exercise is designed to help you learn and gain insight into the factors that may influence you. Self-awareness will enable you to manage your reactions to these triggers more effectively. Triggers can evoke both emotional and physical responses. You will find potential triggers alongside your current response in each row. In the healthy response box, note a more appropriate or healthier response.

Common Triggers	Current Response	Healthy Response
Attitude or Emotion of People Around You		
No Replies/Too Long to Answer Texts/Calls Too Long		
Anniversary Of Significant Date		
Last Minute Change in Plans		
Delays In Plans		

Rushed and Late for a Meeting		
Sudden Change in Social Gathering		
Being Called Out for Making a Mistake		
Sounds or Smells Trigger the Memory		
Relationship Issues/Family Conflict		
A Relationship Ending		
Criticism/Rejection/Feeling Abandoned		

Invalidation in Conversations		
Jokes or Sarcasm that Seem a Personal Attack		
Feeling alone and Isolated		
Feeling Judged or ridiculed		
Financial Burdens		
Feeling Overwhelmed		
(add more)		

GLOBAL SYMPTOM CHECKLIST RATINGS

> **EXERCISE 4.6**: Below are common symptoms that trigger responses in you. This exercise is designed to help you learn and gain insight into the factors that may affect you.
>
> Please rate the symptoms that apply on a scale of 1 to 10 (best) and make notes in the margins that you might note as having significance for you.
>
> *You should consult a physician if you need to, but better safe than sorry.*

Symptoms related to joints and muscles:

- Muscle aches and pains
- Joint pain, stiffness, and swelling
- Muscle weakness
- Inflammation
- List Others:

Symptoms related to the digestive tract:

- Bloating
- Constipation
- Abdominal pain
- Acid reflux
- Nausea
- Food sensitivities
- Blood or mucus in stool (poop)
- List Others:

Symptoms related to the skin:

- Rashes
- Dry eyes
- Dry mouth
- Inflammation
- Hair loss
- Dry skin
- List Others:

Symptoms related to the nervous system:

- Dizziness
- Headaches
- Anxiety and depression
- Confusion and difficulty thinking
- Blurry vision

- Insomnia
- Memory issues
- Migraines
- Lightheadedness
- Numbness and tingling
- List Others:

Physical Symptoms:

- Fatigue
- Pain
- Fever
- Chest pain
- Swollen glands
- Weight gain or loss
- Rapid or irregular heartbeat
- Shortness of breath
- Temperature sensitivity
- List Others:

Symptoms related to mental health

- Suicidal ideation
- Fear
- Self-harm
- Guilt
- Resentment
- Jealousy
- Grief
- Hopelessness
- Helplessness
- Feelings of loneliness
- Isolation
- Sleeplessness
- Depression/sadness
- Negative self-talk
- List Others:

Potential Triggers that Cause Symptoms to Worsen

- Stress
- Medications
- Food
- Hormone changes (period)
- Weather/dry/upbeat/cold/hot
- Flu Shots
- List Other

Miranda's Story

I have struggled with my mental health, moving from service to service and receiving inadequate support for a long time. That left me even more confused about my next steps. I had been diagnosed with anger problems and anxiety. I felt that diagnosis didn't fully reflect what I experienced daily as I read the DSM, and I knew I had Borderline. I've endured depressive episodes and periods of intense anxiety, and my mood was all over the place. I had fears of abandonment, and people hated me. I didn't ask for borderline, but I wanted to feel better and have better relationships with others. I searched tirelessly for help that helped me.

I received a diagnosis of borderline personality disorder (BPD) recently, and I felt liberated. I feel stigmatized by others, like I'm less than for having my disorder. I hate negative judgments. People with borderline personalities face a lot of criticism, I have to say. It depresses me and makes me feel angry.

Though I am now feeling better since I got into treatment, I would like for things to get even better. My BPD impacts my life in every way, every single day. This reality has made bouncing back incredibly challenging at times, but learning to manage and live with BPD is possible. I've begun to observe my BPD rather than get attached and entangled in my troubled emotions and thoughts.

I educated myself and less so by my therapist or psychiatrist, though they can point out unhelpful thought patterns. I felt nobody would do the work I needed to do for me. The work I need to do is care for myself better, but I can't do what I don't know.

When I'm struggling to manage my BPD, I need help, and I found it is better to talk with a therapist rather than family

EXERCISE 4.7 In the space below, what advice would you give to Miranda regarding her situation if she asked? What do you believe could empower her to help herself more effectively?

MODULE FIVE

Managing A Mental Illness Is Challenging but Doable

Module Five Learning Objectives

1. Understand the importance of collaboration, which typically involves open communication, shared decision-making, and a patient-centered approach to treatment.
2. Consider all facets of your health needs that can be effectively met through collaboration with a support system, including your providers.
3. Explore Cognitive Behavioral Therapy (CBT) and Dialectical Behavior Therapy (DBT), which fundamentally operate on the premise that our thoughts, emotions, and behaviors are interconnected.
4. Apply CBT and DBT to effectively transform irrational negative self-talk into more realistic thinking and address emotional dysregulation.
5. Discuss and learn coping skills to manage stress and challenges. Explore how various strategies, including problem-focused and emotion-focused techniques, can be very effective.

A Plan for Living—A Time for Healing

Creating a new life while managing a chronic mental illness is challenging. It's completely normal to experience fear and sadness as you process and live with your condition. However, to gain stability in your life and formulate a plan for living, it's crucial to remember that you aren't alone. This is a time for healing, so surround yourself with people and things that uplift your spirits. Stay connected with healthcare professionals. Building relationships with health providers to guide you through this journey is vital. This might include a medication prescriber, therapist, or social worker.

Overview

The key to long-term stability is safeguarding and sustaining your health as long as possible while also showing resilience in adapting to inevitable life changes. Discuss your ongoing questions and concerns with knowledgeable people who understand you and have your back. Even our best friends may be codependent and may not be good sources of support. Mental health professionals will help you figure out solutions that work for you.

Collaborative Model of Mental Health Care

"Collaboration with care providers" refers to a practice where various healthcare professionals—such as doctors, nurses, therapists, and specialists—work together as a team to coordinate and deliver comprehensive patient care. This approach ensures that all aspects of a patient's health needs are effectively addressed. Collaboration typically involves open communication, shared decision-making, and a patient-centered approach to treatment. It is evaluated by the synergy between providers and patients.

Key aspects of collaboration with care providers:

- **Treatment Teams:** Consist of healthcare professionals from various disciplines, each contributing their unique expertise to the patient's care.
- **Shared goals and objectives:** Establish common patient care goals that all team members work towards
- **Effective communication:** Regular and open communication among all team members, including the patient, keeps everyone informed and on the same page
- **Role clarity:** Understanding each team member's role and responsibilities within the collaborative care process
- **Patient-centered care:** Placing the patient at the center of decision-making and tailoring care plans to their needs

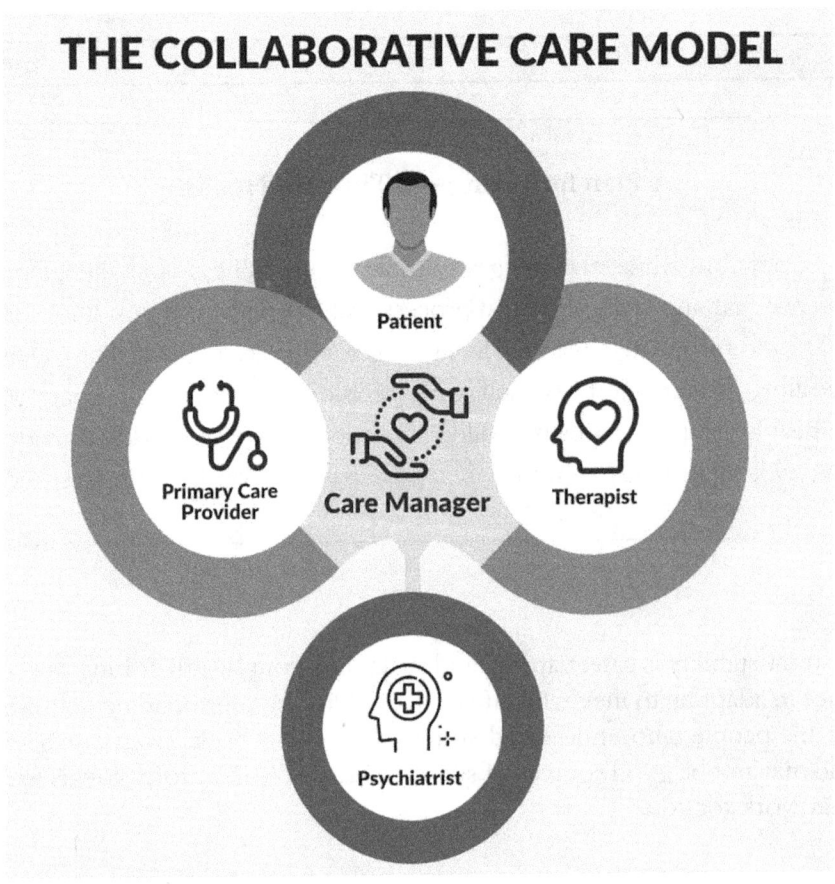

Benefits of collaboration with care providers:

- **Improved quality of care:** Collaborative care can result in more comprehensive and effective treatment plans by integrating diverse perspectives and expertise
- **Reduced medical errors:** Enhanced coordination and communication within a team can help reduce potential mistakes
  Enhanced patient satisfaction: When multiple professionals collaborate, patients feel more supported and involved in their care
- **Optimized resource utilization:** Collaboration prevents unnecessary tests or treatments by coordinating care among different specialties

Examples of collaborative care models:

- **Integrated behavioral health:** Primary care physicians collaborate with mental health professionals to address patients' psychological and physical health needs.
- **Care management teams** consist of healthcare professionals working together to oversee complex chronic conditions through ongoing patient communication and coordination.
- **Patient-centered medical homes:** A primary care model where a team of providers collaborates to deliver coordinated and comprehensive patient care.

The Basics of Collaboration

What has it been like working with your medication prescriber, doctor, therapist, or other healthcare professionals since you became aware that you have BPD?

- What questions could a healthcare provider ask to assist you?
- When your healthcare provider interviews you, they might ask one or more of the following questions: What medications are you currently taking?

Questions your doctor will want you to answer:

- What are your symptoms?
- How severe are your symptoms?
- Have you had to go to the emergency department because of your symptoms?
- How long have you had these symptoms?
- In what ways are your symptoms affecting your quality of life?
- Is there anything that "triggers" your symptoms? Is there anything that worsens them?
- Is there a history of mental illness in your family?

Your mental health providers have similar ethical guidelines that encapsulate the patient's general rights to how we should be treated. Several key principles guide the ACA Code of Ethics 2024:

1. Autonomy: Respecting clients' right to make their own decisions.
2. Nonmaleficence: Avoiding actions that could harm clients.
3. Beneficence: Actively working to promote client well-being.
4. Justice: Ensuring fair and equitable treatment for all clients.

5. Fidelity: Honoring commitments and maintaining trust in professional relationships.
6. Veracity: Practicing honesty and transparency in all professional interactions.

These principles are backed by professional values that emphasize the significance of promoting human development, honoring diversity, championing social justice, safeguarding the counselor-client relationship, and maintaining high standards of competent and ethical practice.

Staying informed about these updates is not just a professional obligation for counseling professionals—it is a commitment to personal growth and excellence in practice. The 2024 Code of Ethics will serve as a vital tool for helping counselors adapt to the evolving needs of their clients and society, ensuring that the counseling profession remains relevant, practical, and firmly grounded in ethical practice.

!!! CAUTION !!!   !!! CAUTION !!!

Though quality of care is important to a patient-centered care. Most providers care, are diligent, and professional, but there are exceptions. In the case of therapists and prescribers, if you don't like the person for whatever reason, you can find another one that matches your desires and needs. However, you may want to be careful spontaneously terminating the relationship between you and the provider. You should discuss this with them if you feel comfortable. As a client or patient, you are likely going to run into many health care professionals. Likely you are going to like some more than others. Ultimately if the provider is competent and adequate communicator than those are excellent qualities to start with.

Medical Errors occur. You should be very mindful of this. Pharmacist and prescribers need to be accountable, but clients need to check the following:

- √ **Double check** the doctors order and prescription. Have them write it down for you.
- √ **Double check** that the prescription matches the one discussed with the prescriber.
- √ **Double check** that the prescription matches the medication bottle.
- √ **Double check** you are taking the dose stated on the medication bottle.

- √ **Talk** with your prescriber when you feel a medication is not working.
- √ **Talk** with your prescriber before you stop your medication.
- √ **Talk** with your prescriber about medication side effect is extreme.

COGNITIVE BEHAVIORAL THERAPY

Cognitive Behavioral Therapy (CBT) fundamentally operates on the premise that our thoughts, emotions, and behaviors are interconnected. This means we can positively influence our feelings and actions by changing our thinking patterns. CBT focuses on identifying and challenging unhelpful thought patterns to develop healthier coping mechanisms and to manage mental health issues by addressing current problems rather than dwelling on the past. It emphasizes practical strategies to enhance daily functioning. A key goal of CBT is to empower individuals to learn how to manage their thoughts and behaviors.

> **EXERCISE 5.1:** Key concepts of CBT. For each CBT concept listed below, describe your experience with it and indicate how bothersome or helpful it may be to you.

- **Cognitive distortions:** Unrealistic or exaggerated negative thoughts—such as all-or-nothing thinking, catastrophizing, and should statements—can cause distress.

- **Automatic thoughts:** Rapid, often negative thoughts that occur automatically in response to a situation.

- **Core beliefs:** Deep-seated assumptions about oneself, the world, and the future that can influence how we interpret situations.

- **Behavioral activation:** Engaging in positive activities to improve mood and counteract negative behaviors.

HOW CBT WORKS

- **Identify negative thought patterns:**

  A therapist or self-help can help you recognize your automatic negative thoughts and how they influence your emotions and behaviors.

- **Challenging negative thoughts:**

  By questioning the validity of these thoughts and considering alternative perspectives, individuals can learn to reframe negative thinking.

- **Developing coping skills:**

  Learning strategies to manage difficult emotions and situations, such as relaxation techniques, problem-solving skills, and assertiveness training.

- **Behavioral experiments:**

  Testing out new behaviors to see how they impact thoughts and feelings.

Important Aspects of CBT

- **Collaborative approach:**
  CBT is a collaborative process in which the therapist partners with the individual to identify and address problems.

- **Focus on the present:**
  CBT mainly emphasizes present thoughts and behaviors instead of exploring past experiences.

- **Education and self-management:**

Tamika's Story

Growing up, I didn't realize I had borderline personality disorder (BPD), but I felt that something was "wrong." Throughout my childhood and young adult years, I struggled with the ups and downs of relationships with friends and family. I was often labeled as "hysterical," quick to anger, and manipulative. One moment, I could like someone, but then they could make a minor mistake, and my perception of them would shatter. I ended many friendships poorly and lost even more due to my unpredictable behavior.

I often say that I've struggled with mental health challenges my entire life. I can't recall when I wasn't sad, and my parents also can't remember when I was just a happy-go-lucky child. Most of my childhood memories involve instances where I felt incredibly upset, angry, jealous, resentful, or depressed. I often felt left out.

During this time, I also fought an eating disorder and dealt with suicidal thoughts. I ended up in the hospital and went through three or four intensive outpatient programs. My mood and behavior were unpredictable, causing concern for many around me. Depression, anxiety, and eating disorders run in my family, but my parents hoped this was just a phase I would outgrow.

My mom wanted me to start therapy and see a psychiatrist, but even when I agreed to go, I soon changed my mind and felt angry at the thought of needing help. I was diagnosed with depression, and then a few years later, I received a diagnosis of anorexia nervosa, but my main problem is BPD. I felt some satisfaction in receiving these diagnoses, as I had struggled to understand my mental health for years.

Learning that I have BPD made me feel hopeless. However, I was finally relieved to understand what was wrong with me. I have been working hard to maintain my health, and I receive support from my friends, doctors, and therapists. I collaborate with my doctor and therapist on my treatment, which has been very helpful. I am now on the right path to helping myself.

I am genuinely interested in joining everyone who has BPD to eliminate the stigma surrounding it. Moving forward, one of my life goals is to help de-stigmatize individuals with BPD and encourage everyone to seek help. Support is available. We are not bad people; we think differently, and that's perfectly fine because we all work hard to stay healthy. I am proud of the journey that has brought me here. Without it, I wouldn't be who I am today!

EXERCISE 5.2: Provide your response to Tamicka's story in the space below? In what ways do you connect to her experiences?

NEGATIVE SELF-TALK

By questioning the validity of these thoughts and considering alternative perspectives, individuals can learn to reframe negative thinking. **Negative self-talk** is a common occurrence among patients with mental illness. Adjusting to this way of life can be psychologically exhausting, prompting many people to seek cognitive behavioral therapy to change the repetitive, negative thought patterns that underlie their depression. You may have distorted views of yourself, but CBT and a skilled therapist can help you detach from these opposing views and replace them with more realistic and constructive self-appraisals.

CBT is effective in transforming irrational, negative self-talk into more realistic thinking.

Thinking positively or neutrally has a positive influence on our health. These mindsets affect our emotions. If you're telling yourself a positive message, a common example is:

"I am not good enough—I am good enough."

"I am dumb—No, that's dumb. I am smart/pretty/interesting."

"I hate myself—STOP...I am working on myself, and I am a good person."

You may not *feel* your best or have a positive outlook. Transforming our unhelpful thoughts into constructive ones is essential for improving our feelings. Constructive thinking asks you to step back without judgment and in a fair and balanced manner. For example:

Unhelpful and unrealistic thought	More realistic and balanced thought
I always screw things up, I'm such a loser. What's wrong with me?	Everyone makes mistakes, including me – I'm only human. All I can do now is try my best to fix the situation and learn from this experience.
I can't do it. I hate myself. Why do people hate me?	STOP! I can do it if I try. I am resilient and persistent, look at what I have been through. I do a good job caring for myself. I'm a hard worker and a good mom.

ASSIGNMENT 5.3: Challenging Negative Self-Talk

What negative self-talk runs through your head? What statements or distortions do you frequently make? Please write at least three negative self-talk statements below or in your journal. Then, for each example you provide, create a positive self-statement that challenges and counters it.

For example, a.) "I am stupid…" correction; b.) I'm smart and know how to do things. The idea that I am stupid comes from childhood trauma resulting from my parents humiliating me. Nobody is trying to shame me now, but the situation reminds me of this. I am reminded to stop treating myself with disrespect.

Unhelpful and unrealistic thought	More realistic and balanced thought
I always screw things up, I'm such a loser. What's wrong with me?	Everyone makes mistakes, including me – I'm only human. All I can do now is try my best to fix the situation and learn from this experience.
I can't do it. I feel way too anxious. Why can't I control my anxiety?	It's OK and normal to feel anxious. It's not dangerous, and it doesn't have to stop me. I can feel anxious and STILL go to the party.

MY SUPPORT SYSTEM

Living with a mental illness can feel isolating. Feelings of isolation, mental health challenges, and various limitations make it difficult to connect with others and receive the support you need. That's why it's crucial to surround yourself with a support network, including personal and professional resources. We are lucky to have so much information and support available online, such as Facebook and X.

EXERCISE 5.4: My Support System: Friends and family are often helpful, while others are not. This exercise will help you to gain insight into how supportive the people around you are.

Make a list of people who are supportive of you.

Which of your family, friends, or coworkers often triggers you, and why? How can you set boundaries in this situation?

Physical and mental self-care

Both mental illnesses and chronic health conditions benefit from reduced stress, better sleep, and adherence to medical providers' treatment recommendations. Dietary changes and exercise can often contribute to an overall improvement in these conditions.

Getting enough sleep is the most important thing anyone can do, especially for those with a mental illness. Plan your schedule to avoid taking on too much. Meditation and exercise help tremendously. You might feel better when listening to soft music or when it rains. We all need to learn to honor our bodies' need for rest. You'll also find peace knowing you are more than your diagnosis. You are valuable, you matter, and you are a person deserving of love.

> *Changes in a person's sleep cycle may signal that the symptoms of your illness could worsen. Sleep is the most vital element for sustaining health and well-being.*

EXERCISE 5.5: Assessing Your Sleep Habits

1) How would you describe your sleep habits in less than eight words?

2)

3) How much do you sleep every day?

4) Where do you usually sleep?

5) Is your sleep uninterrupted?

6) Do you feel anxious or have unwanted or obsessive thoughts that accompany your sleeplessness? Describe and explain what is going on when this occurs.

7) Is there anything else interfering with your sleep?

8) What changes can you make to get eight hours of sleep?

HEALTHY COPING STRATEGIES

This section discusses coping skills for managing stress and challenges. It examines how various strategies can be highly effective, including problem-focused and emotion-focused techniques.

Maintaining healthy coping skills is essential for navigating challenging times, whether facing a problematic parent, a child, neighbors, a demanding job, or limited personal time. Coping skills help you endure, reduce, and effectively manage stress and challenging situations, enhancing your life.

Coping skills are strategies for managing stressful situations. Effectively handling stress can boost physical and mental health and improve one's ability to perform at best.

Some coping strategies that offer quick relief can be tempting, but these may lead to more serious issues later. Developing healthy coping skills is essential for alleviating emotional stress and effectively managing the stressful situations you encounter. Examples of healthy coping skills include:

- Establishing and maintaining boundaries
- Practicing relaxation strategies such as deep breathing, meditation, and mindfulness
- Engaging in regular physical activity
- Making to-do lists and setting goals

> *Healthy boundaries* are essential, yet many people struggle to maintain them.

Best practices for establishing and maintaining healthy boundaries include identifying your needs and limits, communicating them assertively to others, consistently upholding those boundaries, learning to say "no" when necessary, and actively reflecting on your boundaries to ensure they remain effective. This may involve setting physical boundaries, managing social media interactions, and seeking support when needed.

There are several types of boundaries, including physical, emotional, sexual, material, and time boundaries. These boundaries can help people feel safe and comfortable in their relationships.

Here are several types of boundaries:

Physical boundaries:
- People respecting your personal space, physical touch, respect for privacy, and preferences for closeness.

Emotional boundaries
- How much and when to share personal information
- Respect for others' emotional needs
- How to handle your own and others' emotions

Sexual boundaries
- Ask for consent, check in with your partner's comfort level, and talk about sexual matters.

Material and financial boundaries
- How do you treat your belongings, treat others' belongings, and spend your money?

Time boundaries
- How to balance work and personal time
- How to set aside time for self-care
- How to respect others' time

Intellectual boundaries
- How to share your thoughts and ideas, respect others' ideas, and be aware of appropriate discussion topics.

TYPES OF BOUNDARIES

PHYSICAL
Protect my personal space & body

EMOTIONAL
Protect my thoughts & feelings

VERBAL
Protect how we speak & what we discuss

TIME
Protect how I spend my time

WORK
Protect my limits in the workplace

SPIRITUAL
Protect my values & what I believe in

FINANCIAL
Protect my finances & assets

SEXUAL
Protect my safety & preferences

How to Establish and Maintain Boundaries

- √ **Express your needs:** Articulate your needs and expectations in relationships while staying receptive to the needs of others. However, this can be more challenging than it seems, as effective communication requires at least two individuals to be willing to collaborate.

- √ **Saying No:** Assertively decline without fear of rejection. The truth is that some people may not accept your 'no' and could choose to walk away. That reflects on them and does not diminish your value or worth. If you establish and consistently maintain boundaries, most people will initially test those limits to see if you're serious. They will hear your 'no' and respect it if you are.

- √ **Set boundaries for yourself. Ensure accountability in critical areas of your life, such as finances, mental health, and work.** Create limits for time management, such as using a timer during meetings.

- √ **Taking responsibility:** Own your emotions and reactions.

- √ **Setting physical boundaries:** Ask others to respect your personal space or communicate how you want them to interact with your belongings.

- √ **Establish digital boundaries.** Limit your time online, especially on social media. These platforms can be unsafe environments where various forms of exploitation occur. If using social media feels stressful, it likely is, particularly if you actively engage with it. We recommend against sharing your passwords with social media followers.

- √ **Establishing emotional boundaries is essential.** You need to prioritize what makes you feel safe. However, your emotional boundaries could be unhealthy for you and for intimate relationships in general.

- √ **Set boundaries with your** child. Encourage them to wait, practice patience, or let them know you need some space.

- √ **Set boundaries with your roommates.** Encourage them to ask for permission before using your belongings.

- √ **Setting boundaries with sexual partners.** Communicate your preferences and dislikes clearly to your partner.

Here are some phrases you can use to set boundaries:

- "I can't do that, but here's what I can do instead."
- "I understand where you're coming from, but I must say no."
- "This is what I'm comfortable with."

- "I need us to respect each other's time."
- "I need you to respect my decision."

Examples of boundary setting:

- "I need some time alone right now; can we talk later?" (Setting a time boundary)
- "I'm not comfortable discussing that topic" (Setting a topic boundary)
- "I prefer not to be contacted after a certain hour" (Setting a communication boundary)

EXERCISE 5.6: IT'S OKAY TO SAY "NO."

Establishing boundaries for your mental health begins by identifying your limits and needs and then communicating those boundaries to others using assertive language. Consistently uphold them by saying "no" when necessary and prioritizing self-care to protect your well-being. This entails recognizing when your boundaries are crossed and addressing the situation directly.

Please write several boundary-setting statements you currently use and those you would like to adopt in the future in the space below. For each statement you identify, describe the situation in which you might to use it.

1.)

2.)

3.)

COPING SKILLS AND TECHNIQUES

Coping skills are techniques and tools that assist individuals in managing difficult emotions and stress, allowing them to maintain a sense of order and balance. They can improve well-being when people feel anxious, sad, angry, or overwhelmed.

What are coping skills used for?

- **Managing emotions**

Coping skills can help people manage their feelings and reduce negative emotions

- **Reducing stress**

Coping skills can help people reduce stress and feel more in control of their situation

- **Building resilience**

Coping skills can help individuals build resilience, which is the capacity to adapt effectively to adversity

What are some examples of coping skills?

- **Problem-focused**

Addressing the problem that is causing distress, such as planning, active coping, and restraint coping

- **Emotion-focused**

Reducing negative emotions associated with the problem, such as positive reframing, acceptance, humor, and turning to religion

- **Social coping**

Looking for emotional or practical support from others, like chatting with a friend, joining a support group, or getting professional help

- **Physical coping**

Engaging in physical activities to release stress and stay emotionally balanced, such as deep breathing, mindful stretching, walking meditations, or regular exercise

How can coping skills be used?

- Coping skills can be applied in the moment, particularly when angry or overwhelmed

- Coping skills can be integrated into your daily routine by going to bed at a reasonable hour, eating healthily, and connecting with friends and family

---

Two types of coping skills are problem-based coping and emotion-based coping. Understanding how they differ can help you determine your best coping strategy.

TWO TYPES OF COPING

Problem-Focused Coping	Emotion-Focused Coping
Problem-Focused Coping	Social Support
Emotion-Focused Coping	Distraction With Pleasurable Activities
Problem Solving	Talking With a Friend
Getting Organized	Diaphragmatic Breathing
Time-Management	Relaxation
Assertive Communication	Mindfulness
Social Support	Emotional Support

- **Problem-focused coping** is effective when you need to change your circumstances, such as by removing a stressful event from your life. For example, if you are in an unhealthy relationship, ending it (rather than simply calming your emotions) may be the best way to reduce your anxiety and sadness.

- **Emotion-based coping** is beneficial when you need to process your feelings without attempting to change your situation or when circumstances are beyond your control. For instance, if you are mourning the loss of a loved one, it is vital to address your emotions healthily since you cannot alter the situation.

There isn't always one best way to proceed. Instead, it's up to you to determine which coping skill will be most effective for your situation. Below are examples of stressful scenarios and how each approach could be utilized.

Healthy Emotion-Focused Coping Skills

Whether you're feeling lonely, nervous, sad, or angry, emotion-focused coping skills can assist you in healthily managing your feelings. Effective coping strategies may soothe, temporarily distract or help you cope with your distress.

While using coping skills is essential for relieving some of your distress, these strategies shouldn't be solely about distracting you from reality. In other situations, coping skills can help improve your mood. If you've had a tough day at work, playing with your kids or watching a funny movie can lift your spirits. Alternatively, if you're feeling angry about something someone said, a healthy coping strategy might help you calm down before reacting in a way you might regret.

Other examples of healthy ways to cope with emotions include:

- **Take care of yourself**: Be kind and forgiving to yourself. Set aside time for self-care. Use lotion with a pleasant fragrance, spend time in nature, listen to music, cleanse your space with sage, light a candle, indulge in a bath, sip tea, or treat your body in ways that make you feel good, such as painting your nails, styling your hair, and applying a face mask.

- **Engage in a hobby**: Explore enjoyable activities like coloring, drawing, solving puzzles, reading, journaling, or listening to music.

- **Exercise**: Any physical activity is essential for health. You can do yoga, walk, or play a recreational sport.

- **Focus on a task**: Clean up the house (or a closet, drawer, or specific area), prepare a meal, tend to the garden, or enjoy reading a book.

- **Practice mindfulness** by recognizing what you are grateful for, meditating, visualizing your "happy place," or viewing pictures that remind you of the people, places, and things that bring you joy.

- **Use relaxation strategies**: Play with a pet, practice breathing exercises, squeeze a stress ball, use a relaxation app, enjoy some aromatherapy, or write in a journal.

Healthy Problem-Focused Coping Skills

You can confront a problem directly and remove the source of your stress in various ways. Sometimes, this might involve altering your behavior or developing a plan clarifying your actions.

Problem-focused coping may involve more significant actions in different situations, such as changing jobs or ending a relationship. Here are some examples of practical problem-focused coping skills:

- Ask for support from a friend or a professional
- Create a to-do list
- Engage in problem-solving
- Establish and enforce healthy boundaries
- Walk away and leave a situation that is causing you stress
- Work on managing your time better

UNHEALTHY COPING SKILLS TO AVOID

Just because a strategy helps you deal with emotional pain doesn't mean it's healthy. Some coping skills can lead to more significant problems in your life. Here are some examples of unhealthy coping skills:

- **Drinking alcohol or using drugs** may temporarily numb your pain, but they won't resolve your problems. Instead, they are likely to introduce new challenges into your life. For example, alcohol is a depressant that can worsen your feelings of distress. Relying on substances for coping increases your risk of developing a substance use disorder and can lead to health, legal, financial, and social difficulties. Substance abuse heightens the risk of suicide or premature health-related deaths and often results in criminal behavior, prosecution, and incarceration. That's no fun for anyone.

- **Overeating**: Food is a common coping mechanism for women more often than for men. However, emotional eating—often described as "stuffing your feelings" with food—can result in an unhealthy relationship with food and various health problems. Sometimes, individuals may swing to the opposite extreme and limit their eating to feel more in control.

- **Sleeping too much or too little**: Whether you nap when stressed or sleep in to avoid confronting the day, sleep offers a brief escape from your problems. However, when you wake up, the issue will still be there.

- **Venting to others**: Sharing your problems can help you gain support, find solutions, or gain fresh perspectives, which can be beneficial. However, a person with a mental illness might sometimes feel overwhelmed by the listener. It's important to share your feelings with a few trusted individuals. Additionally, if you find yourself obsessively venting about the same issue, it may indicate that you're feeling stuck, suggesting a need to discuss this with a professional. Studies show that continuously venting about how bad your situation is or how terrible you feel is more likely to keep you in a state of pain.

- **Overspending**: While many assert that they enjoy "retail therapy" to boost their spirits, shopping can become detrimental. Unnecessary expenses jeopardize overall financial stability. Often, individuals spend money they do not possess, leading to a financial crisis that affects not only themselves but also their family members.

- **Avoidance**: Even so-called "healthy" coping strategies can become unhealthy if used to escape problems. For example, when you're stressed about your financial situation, you might feel tempted to spend time with friends or watch TV because it seems less anxiety-inducing than working on a budget. However, if you never confront your financial issues, your coping strategies will only mask the problem, and eventually, this situation will overwhelm you. Your mental health can suffer during periods of economic stress.

- **Engaging in unhealthy sexual behaviors** or sex addiction often requires validation through sexual acting out. Promiscuity frequently serves to enter a fleeting relationship for validation or to avoid forming deeper attachments. Additionally, it is often preferable to end a relationship rather than be the one who is left. Individuals with BPD tend to fear attachment, worrying that abandonment is inevitable. This can lead to a perpetual cycle of self-sabotaging behaviors.

Jared's Story

I am 26 years old and live with my mother because I need help getting by. I was diagnosed with BPD about three years ago. When I learned what it was, I researched everything I could. I was excited because all my problems finally had an explanation, and maybe I wasn't such a bad person after all. Perhaps it wasn't entirely my fault, as I had always been told and believed. Most importantly, maybe I had a chance to get better.

Unfortunately, a few years later, the societal stigma surrounding mental illness reared its ugly head. People started saying that I was using my diagnosis as an excuse for my behavior. Most of my family doesn't believe my diagnosis, and every friend I made left during those brief periods when I couldn't control my emotions. I can't blame them for not wanting to be around me, but this has left me with no support system. I feel there is no hope because no one wants to help. Not someone like me. Not someone with questionable actions in their past.

Imagine the most intense feeling you've ever experienced. I often sense an unbearable depth of emotion. However, when I panic or fall in love, that intensity multiplies tenfold, making me feel like I'm drowning. My emotions can quickly become overwhelming, consuming me entirely. Consequently, I act in ways I deeply regret, yet I must live with the shame of my actions. People don't truly understand me.

I often feel hopeless and helpless. There's nothing I can do to change it. I can't get close to anyone because I love them too much, and they inevitably hurt me in one way or another. Then, I overreact and say or do something that pushes them away. They call me toxic, and I agree. My self-esteem is terrible. A lack of emotional control leads me to ruin my relationships, causing people to walk away due to my abandonment issues. It's a cycle of negativity.

EXERCISE 5.7 Reflect on Jared's situation and story.

Please write a few sentences restating the issues Jared faces:

Please share some advice and support with Jared. Can this support be applied to you?

Reflect on your thoughts when reading Jared's s

Cognitive Behavioral Therapy is the Foundation for Dialectical Behavioral Therapy

Psychologist Aaron Beck developed cognitive therapy in the 1960s. This treatment is founded on the principle that maladaptive behavior (ineffective, self-defeating behavior) is triggered by inappropriate or irrational thinking patterns known as automatic thoughts.

Therapists, mental health coaches, and educators use various techniques during cognitive therapy to help individuals examine their thoughts and behaviors. Self-help enthusiasts can do this independently, though recognizing unproductive statements may be out of their awareness. The CBT strategies are evidence-based, meaning their positive effects are demonstrated and supported by research and scientific studies. We have incorporated these techniques into this training; anyone can use them if they find them beneficial on their healing journeys. This workbook was developed to assist you in integrating the strategies into your life.

Strategies and Techniques include:

- ***Validity testing.*** In this stage, you reflect on, defend, and evaluate your thoughts and beliefs in a specific scenario. This aligns with what we discussed in an earlier section.

  Examples:
  - A person believes, "I'm going to fail this presentation," before giving a speech at work.
  - The therapist, friend, or significant other might ask, "Can you recall past presentations where you performed well? What evidence supports the idea that this presentation will be different?"

- ***Cognitive rehearsal*** assists individuals in visualizing challenging situations they have faced, enabling them to practice coping strategies effectively. When they encounter a similar situation again, they can apply the rehearsed behaviors to manage it. This therapeutic technique involves imagining oneself performing a task. It can enhance performance, reduce anxiety, and boost self-confidence.

  Examples:
  - *People with social anxiety:* Imagining a conversation or social interaction before an event.
  - *People with interpersonal difficulties* might imagine that an upcoming difficult discussion will occur. The person rehearses healthy responses in their mind.
  - *People with phobias or anxiety disorders* can benefit from visualizing anxiety-inducing situations and repeating positive coping statements.

- ***Cognitive rehearsal*** effectively addresses anxiety and promotes healthy responses. Here's how cognitive rehearsal works.
  1. Identify scenarios that trigger undesired reactions

2. Visualize the scenario as vividly and realistically as possible
3. Pay attention to thoughts, emotions, and actions
4. Repeat the rehearsal to become more comfortable and confident

- *Guided discovery:* You can ask questions to help you identify unhelpful, destructive, and unhealthy thoughts and behaviors. This technique highlights aspects you might overlook, such as cognitive distortions.

Example:

Explore the idea: "What leads me to believe that others will judge you so harshly?" Examine the evidence: reflect on past situations where the client felt judged and assess the outcomes.

Thought process: "I often feel like a failure when I make mistakes at work."

Inner response: "Can I recall a time when I made a mistake at work that didn't define me as a failure? What occurred in that situation?"

- *Journaling.* We recommend keeping a detailed diary of daily situations, including the thoughts and emotions accompanying them and the behaviors that arise. Separately from group work, the therapist and patient review the journal to identify maladaptive thought patterns and how these thoughts influence behavior.

- *Homework.* You may be asked to complete assignments that encourage self-discovery and reinforce insights gained in therapy or those that come to you alone. These tasks might include note-taking, journaling, reviewing an audio recording of your therapy session, or reading books or articles relevant to your progress for your benefit. You will focus on applying a newly learned strategy or coping mechanism to a situation and documenting the results for your next therapy session.

- *Modeling.* Role-playing exercises enable the therapist to demonstrate suitable responses to various situations.

- *Schema-focused therapy.* This therapy, developed by Dr. Jeffrey Young, a psychologist at Columbia University, is based on the premise that BPD patients have four maladaptive life schemas (world views that originate in childhood): "abandoned/abused child," "angry/impulsive child," "detached protector," and "punitive parent." The goal of therapy is to help the patient shed these schemas and instead adopt a new mode of behavior, that of the "healthy adult." Therapists focus on building the therapeutic relationship and use techniques such as guided imagery, assertiveness training, and role playing to help the patient confront daily experiences and past traumatic events.

DIALECTICAL BEHAVIOR THERAPY WORKS

Dialectical Behavior Therapy (DBT) provides both theoretical and empirical insights. It consists of various stages that promote a willingness to improve and develop healthy coping skills. DBT is a practical therapeutic approach that assists individuals in learning the skills and strategies necessary for a fulfilling life. Initially developed as a treatment for individuals with BPD experiencing suicidal tendencies or self-harming behaviors, DBT is rooted in cognitive behavior therapy, which aims to identify harmful or ineffective thought patterns so individuals can work toward change. It's termed "dialectical" because it merges the seemingly opposing ideas of acceptance and change, suggesting that integrating both concepts is more helpful than relying on either alone.

For individuals dealing with serious psychological issues, managing them can become increasingly difficult without engaging in some form of therapy. In addition to treating Borderline Personality Disorder, Dialectical Behavior Therapy, and expressive arts therapy also help address the following disorders:

- Mood disorders, including depression
- Anxiety disorders
- Eating disorders, such as anorexia and bulimia
- Substance abuse
- Other personality disorders, such as Dependent Personality Disorder

Many of the disorders mentioned earlier are associated with a variety of behavioral issues that DBT is specifically intended to address. Through its different phases, Dialectical Behavior Therapy empowers individuals facing these disorders to tackle challenges such as emotional dysregulation, impulsivity, and self-harming behaviors.

What Is the Evidence Behind DBT?

Marsha Linehan, PhD, originally developed Dialectical Behavior Therapy to help female patients whose suicidal tendencies were not adequately addressed by traditional therapies. Given that approximately 75 percent of those diagnosed with borderline personality disorder (BPD) attempt suicide at least once.

A study conducted by the National Institute of Mental Health found that Dialectical Behavior Therapy was ***twice as effective as other therapies*** in reducing suicide attempts among individuals diagnosed with borderline personality disorder, and it also led to a decrease of more than fifty percent in emergency room visits.

DBT is not only effective for BPD. Studies have demonstrated that DBT can significantly reduce anger, depression, self-harm, disordered eating behaviors, and feelings of hopelessness. When applied to substance abuse, DBT can lessen urges to use, cravings, and physical discomfort from abstaining.

In addition to helping treat various disorders, Dialectical Behavior Therapy can teach you healthier coping skills to help you maintain your recovery and improve your quality of life.

The term "dialectical" is not used in the strict sense that a philosopher might employ. Instead, it refers to an approach aimed at reconciling apparent contradictions—such as acknowledging a patient's perspective while promoting change. Dialectical behavior therapy typically lasts about a year and includes group and individual sessions. In group therapy, patients learn more constructive behaviors and responses through sessions focused on problem-solving, mindfulness meditation, muscle relaxation, and breath training. In individual psychotherapy (often supplemented by telephone coaching), the therapist aids the patient in integrating lessons from group sessions into their daily life.

Studies conducted by researchers at the University of Washington have concluded that dialectical behavior therapy is effective in reducing self-harm and suicide attempts, as well as the number of days spent in psychiatric hospitals. In one study involving 101 women with BPD who had attempted suicide at least twice in the previous five years, the investigators randomly assigned half to receive dialectical behavior therapy and the other half to treatment from expert clinicians (defined as experienced and affiliated with prestigious institutions). Both interventions lasted for one year. The researchers found that patients who received dialectical behavior therapy were half as likely as the others to attempt suicide and were less likely to engage in self-harm or require hospitalization.

In another study, researchers at the University of Amsterdam randomly assigned 58 women with BPD to receive either dialectical behavior therapy or standard treatment. After one year of therapy, those receiving dialectical behavior therapy were less likely to self-harm or engage in other impulsive, self-destructive behaviors compared to those receiving standard care. Six months after the intervention ended, dialectical behavior therapy demonstrated greater effectiveness than standard treatment.

FOUR ELEMEENTS OF THE DBT MODEL

Some examples of DBT skills include:

- **Mindfulness** involves being present in the moment and observing your thoughts and feelings without judgment.
- **Distress tolerance** involves learning to manage intense emotions without resorting to self-harm or destructive behaviors.
- **Emotion regulation** involves learning to recognize, label, and adjust your responses to challenging emotions.
- **Interpersonal effectiveness** involves learning to communicate assertively and resolve conflicts.

The DBT learning path is divided into four phases based on Linehan's clinical and research work:

I. **Stage one:** Linehan's paradigm's fundamental, unspoken goal is **to enhance self-control**. This initial stage of DBT establishes the foundation for your success. During this stage, you will begin learning how to manage your behaviors, including those that prevent you from receiving necessary help or that lead to self-harm, whether physical or emotional. You will also work with a therapist or independently identify any additional disorders that may coincide with your primary disorder.

II. **Stage two:** A person with BPD learns to self-express healthily. Rather than bottling up emotional responses, stage two of DBT highlights the importance of expressing emotions. By sharing your feelings, you can learn to manage underlying issues and protect your physical and mental health. In this stage, you will work with your therapist or independently to recognize and process any traumatic experiences or emotional challenges that have hindered your ability to overcome past obstacles.

III. **Stage three:** DBT focuses on teaching self-control, expression, and problem-solving. By combining the skills developed in the first two stages of DBT, you will use this stage to learn how to effectively solve your problems while striving to maintain proper functioning in your life.

IV. **Stage Four:** In the final stage of the DBT process, therapists work with you to help you reconnect with the important people in your life. You can learn how to cultivate positive relationships during this last phase of therapy by **developing communication skills and addressing potential attachment and detachment issues**.

During these stages, you will concentrate on developing skills in emotional regulation, distress tolerance, mindfulness, and interpersonal effectiveness.

MINDFULNESS AND GRATITUDE

More psychiatrists, psychologists, and other mental health professionals have begun integrating mindfulness meditation training into their psychotherapy practices in the last decade. Mindfulness meditation can positively impact a variety of mental health conditions, including major depressive disorder, bipolar disorder, schizophrenia, borderline personality disorder, chronic pain, and generalized anxiety disorder. This training may assist individuals with mental illness in developing effective coping skills during emotional distress. Mindfulness techniques create a moment of space to acknowledge emotions and foster a more thoughtful way of responding to those emotions.

What Is Mindfulness Meditation?

Mindfulness meditation focuses on being present in the moment without judging others and being intentional.

When practicing mindfulness meditation, you focus on being present rather than thinking about the past or future. You cultivate an awareness of your surroundings, including sensations related to what you see, smell, and touch.

Because mindfulness is about not judging, you must practice thinking of these things neutrally.

What Does Mindfulness Meditation Have to Do with Mental Illness?

Marsha Linehan, Ph.D., who developed DBT, was among the pioneers to incorporate mindfulness meditation training in treating BPD. Individuals with BPD and other mental illnesses often feel intense emotions and may become "stuck" in these feelings.

Unfortunately, judging an emotion—whether it's yours or someone else's—can intensify that feeling. Judgmental thoughts can also introduce additional emotions; for instance, if you tell yourself you're weak for feeling sad, you may experience both sadness and shame.

Mindfulness meditation training may help individuals with mental illness more effectively utilize healthy coping strategies for emotional pain. Mindfulness skills enable you to create a little space for recognizing an emotion and responding more thoughtfully.

For example, imagine having a verbal argument with someone you love. You might experience intense emotions during the argument, such as anger, fear, and rage. Without mindfulness skills, you're more likely to act on these feelings without considering the consequences. You may yell at your loved one, throw something, or storm out.

With mindfulness meditation practice, you may be able to notice your emotions, step back, and choose your behavior appropriately, such as taking a break until you can discuss things quietly.

What are other mental health and educational applications for Mindfulness?

Mindfulness is a practice that involves being aware of the present moment without judgment. It can help reduce stress and relax the body and mind.

What are the components of mindfulness?

- *Intention:* Choosing to be more aware
- *Attention:* Focusing on the present moment, thoughts, and sensations
- *Attitude:* Being curious, kind, and non-judgmental

How can you practice mindfulness?

- **Focus on your breath**

Notice how your breath moves in and out of your nostrils and how it feels as it rises and falls in your chest and belly

- **Observe your thoughts**

When you notice your mind has wandered, gently bring your attention back to your breath

- **Practice regularly**

Set aside time to practice mindfulness or try to incorporate it into your daily life

- **Find resources**

Look for mindfulness classes, books, or programs in your community

What are some benefits of mindfulness?

- Mindfulness can help reduce stress
- It can help you be more aware of your surroundings
- It can help you be more present and engaged in what's happening in the moment

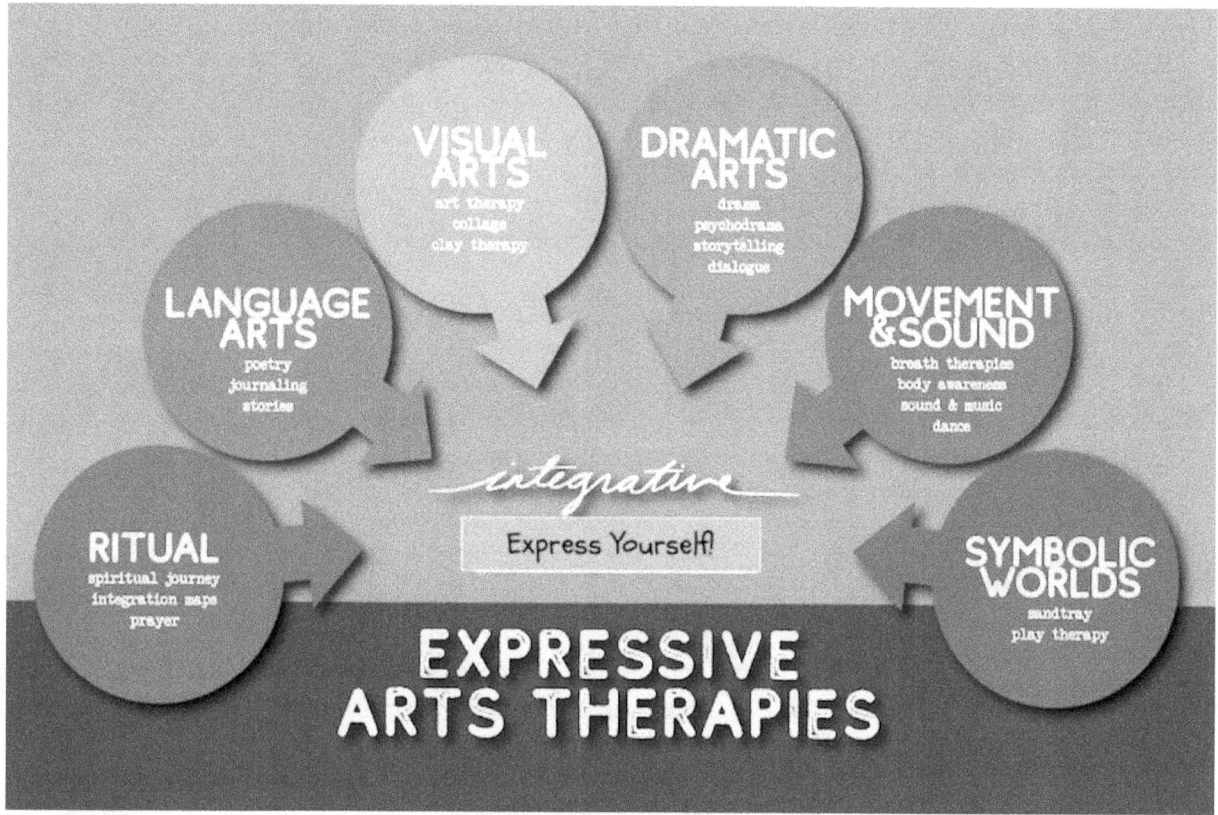

Constructivist theory integrates narrative and other expressive art therapies. We encourage clients to embrace their authentic selves, empowering them to take control of their life stories. In existential theory, authenticity and vulnerability are interconnected with self-compassion, self-awareness, responsibility, and freedom (Hoffman 2009; Yalom 2009).

Competing Myths or Stories People Tell, and We Believe About Us

Expressing yourself enables meaningful communication that nurtures positive self-understanding and self-worth. Others share stories that derive meaning from the myths they currently embrace, or they discuss these myths (May 1992). These definitions, often imposed on us, are indeed myths. Hoffman states, "Myths represent the universality of the existential givens and the particularity of cultural responses to those givens" (2009, p. 26). Myths are narratives about us that are generally untrue yet widely accepted as accurate.

Expression and self-awareness beyond existing limitations include emotional and cognitive elements. This may involve the client's inventive use of artistic mediums to foster therapeutic change. Typically, this encompasses movement, drama, and music therapy but also integrates visual art and writing. In terms of writing, this might involve poetry, short stories, journaling, memoirs, essays, vignettes, letters, song lyrics, freewriting, reports, speeches, blogs, video essays, and vlogs. Research has shown that expressive art interventions are more effective when they include experiential awareness of client issues (Feder & Feder, 1981).

Expression is Liberation

We add that achieving "liberation" from internal oppression through expressive forms involves sharing creative work with others. Can we truly be liberated if our creative work is never shared? According to West-Olatunji and Rush-Ossenbeck, "A central practice of expressive art counseling is allowing clients to experience and define themselves beyond conventional limitations. The liberating concept of this approach to counseling is reinforced by the idea that the client's self-expression is often stifled by some form of suffering" (2016, 425). Suffering is released through the act of expression and sharing it with others. As a result, healing takes place.

Resist and deconstruct old stories about you

Therefore, participants using these approaches might create stories that "resist" and "deconstruct" the old narratives imposed on them by themselves, their families, and the community (Psychotherapy.net, 2011). Consequently, clients influence and are influenced by those around them. This situation is particularly problematic for individuals with mental illnesses, as they often perceive others as gaslighting them and attempting to define them in unflattering and offensive ways.

Self-constructed narratives empower individuals with mental illness to define themselves consistently and coherently. Artistic creation encourages clients to externalize their challenges. Stories assist clients in processing, understanding, and gaining perspective on the "psychic pain" often linked to illness, trauma, and difficult events in their lives. Clients build more beneficial narratives about themselves. This may involve "de-stigmatizing" their identities and developing a more accepting and authentic view of themselves, fostering acceptance and creating healthier definitions of who they are. Narrative therapy is a vital component of this therapeutic program.

When you express yourself creatively, it feels liberating

When you express yourself, you will learn to think independently and communicate your ideas responsibly and ethically, exercising your freedom. This element is very empowering for anyone. Both approaches encourage individuals to think autonomously, independent of the community, which might impose definitions and harsh judgments upon them. Journaling and other narrative forms foster self-discovery and expression. They serve as an outlet for painful feelings and emotions, particularly for people with BPD. These methods also create communication channels, especially when shared publicly through publication or in group therapy settings.

Expression involves learning and insight into oneself and problems

In the context of this therapeutic program, sharing can occur either face-to-face or remotely. When individuals become conscious and reflective readers and writers, they can cultivate an openness toward revising their thinking—particularly regarding how they perceive themselves, others, and the world around them. Emotional distance is a significant concept that lacks sufficient articulation in therapy literature. John Garden discussed this idea in his book, *The Art of Fiction*. The simplest way to clarify this concept within writing and healing is that, at some point, the client (writer) gains enough distance from their narrative and character to achieve insight. This insight often emerges because of writing and revision.

Writers often face harsh truths about themselves. This represents the therapeutic arc of narrative therapy. However, as a powerful shaping force, a counselor always maintains neutrality, which I perceive as being present with the clients. Therapists must "listen to understand, allowing time and space for emotional and spiritual issues to arise" (Spillers 2007). Presence in this context includes unconditional positive regard and fostering an environment where clients feel accepted and supported.

Yang (2009) stated, "To be aware of responsibility is to be aware of creating oneself, destiny, life dilemmas, emotions, and if this is the case, one's suffering" (p. 184) and how this intersects with and relates to those around the client. The client must ultimately take responsibility for overcoming barriers that hinder their awareness and authenticity (Hoffman, 2009).

Expressive Creativity Is Empowering

Your creative work represents you, and since you are the author of your own story, it is empowering. You create to transform yourself and leave the old self behind. The purpose of expressive art therapy is to assist clients in gaining more control over their lives by freely expressing their thoughts and feelings. Your voice matters most.

PSYCHODYNAMIC THERAPY

Psychodynamic therapies address unconscious mental processes that originate in childhood and later interfere with the ability to function in adulthood.

Transference-focused psychotherapy is based on the theory initially proposed by Dr. Otto Kernberg, a Weill Medical College of Cornell University psychiatrist. This theory suggests that borderline personality disorder (BPD) arises from "identity diffusion," which is a struggle to reconcile both positive and negative perceptions of oneself and others. This splitting—seeing people and situations as either entirely good or entirely bad—begins in childhood but continues into adulthood, leading to internal turmoil that worsens the symptoms of BPD.

Employing techniques from psychoanalytic psychotherapy, clinicians and patients collaborate to understand the dynamics of past relationships, associated emotions, and their impact on current functioning. Therapy aims to assist patients in better integrating their perceptions of themselves and others. Patients participate in therapy at least twice a week.

Researchers at Cornell randomly assigned 90 patients with BPD to one year of treatment using transference-focused therapy, dialectical behavior therapy, or supportive treatment. They reported results only for the 62 patients who completed at least nine months of treatment. Patients in all three groups showed significant improvement in scores related to depression, anxiety, global functioning, and social functioning. All three interventions were equally effective, but each provided specific advantages.

Both transference-focused therapy and dialectical behavior therapy significantly reduced suicidal behavior, while supportive therapy did not. Additionally, both transference-focused therapy and supportive therapy significantly improved anger. Only transference-focused therapy notably reduced irritability and assaults, both verbal and physical.

Mentalization-based treatment. This therapy, developed by Drs. Peter Fonagy and Anthony Bateman, psychologists at the University of London, is founded on the premise that patients with BPD struggle with their ability to "mentalize" or form a mental representation of their own and others' emotions, feelings, or beliefs. A long-term study found that mentalization-based treatment led to a decrease in antipsychotic use and the number of suicides attempts while also increasing the likelihood of recovery five years after completing treatment.

Since the investigators performed their initial research in a partial hospital setting, they conducted a separate study in an outpatient environment. Over an 18-month study, they randomly assigned 134 patients with BPD to either mentalization-based treatment or structured clinical management, which included case management, supportive counseling, and problem-solving sessions. Although patients in both interventions exhibited notable improvements—measured by reductions in suicide attempts, hospitalizations, and other crisis events—those assigned to mentalization-based treatment showed significantly more significant enhancement compared to those receiving structured clinical management.

Additional Considerations

Although these studies' findings are encouraging, it is crucial to recognize that researchers assessing their therapies have conducted much of the research. A practical consideration is that these psychotherapies require a substantial time commitment from clinicians and patients.

Another option is the Systems Training for Emotional Predictability and Problem Solving (STEPPS) program developed at the University of Iowa. It consists of group treatment for 20 weeks, followed by bi-monthly group therapy for one year. The STEPPS program incorporates cognitive-behavioral techniques and provides guidance on managing emotions. Family members and loved ones are encouraged to attend their sessions to learn how to respond more effectively to a patient with BPD and to reinforce the lessons the patient is learning in group treatment. A review suggested that STEPPS might be a viable alternative when patients cannot commit to more intensive forms of psychotherapy and could serve as an adjunct to other therapies.

Inspirational quotes for People with BPD

Exercise 5.8: Below are two inspirational quotes circulating on the internet that aren't attributed to anyone. Each block has enough space for you to respond to the quotes. 1) Rate the quotes on a scale from 1 to 10, with 10 being the best. 2) Explain why you relate to the quotes in the space provided above or below. 3) Then, in your journal, write down five quotes you create or find elsewhere that fit your circumstances and that you like personally.

"IT'S OKAY NOT TO BE OKAY, BUT IT'S IMPORTANT TO KEEP TRYING."

"You are worthy of love and support, even when you feel your worst."

MODULE SIX

Caring for Your Physical, Mental, and Emotional Health
Developing a Self-Care Plan

Module Six Learning Objectives

1. Understanding self-care empowers you to enhance your health, prevent disease, maintain well-being, and manage illness.
2. Learn the importance of participating in various activities that positively influence your emotional, physical, social, and spiritual well-being.
3. Diminish the effects of negative emotions such as anxiety, stress, anger, and sadness.
4. Explore strategies to maintain balance and foster a sense of purpose and belonging, helping you to achieve your life goals and improve your quality of life.
5. Develop and commit to implementing and revising your Self-Care and Trigger Plans.

Overview

Self-care is a holistic concept, a way of being, and our primary source of vitality. It empowers individuals and families to enhance health, prevent disease, maintain well-being, and manage illness and disability with or without the support of a healthcare provider. Self-care is linked to social involvement and overall wellness. At its core, self-care requires self-discipline, making a certain level of well-being attainable. A person who prioritizes self-care can address their daily and life-related needs.

Self-care contributes to greater life satisfaction.

What Is Self-Care?

The purpose of self-care is to sustain your physical and mental health. You accomplish this by participating in various activities that positively influence your emotional, physical, social, and spiritual well-being. Self-care includes doing things that bring you joy and do not always have to cost anything. Ultimately, it's about participating in activities you enjoy.

We can distinguish several types of self-care:

- **Physical self-care**: Eating well, getting enough sleep, exercising, and taking care of your physical needs
- **Mental self-care**: Practicing self-compassion, self-awareness, and self-reflection
- **Spiritual self-care**: Meditating, spending time in nature, listening to inspirational music, or praying
- **Social self-care**: Having healthy relationships
- **Self-care activities**: Taking a bath, reading a book, going for a walk, or doing a craft

Self-care can help you:

- Promote and maintain health
- Manage a chronic illness
- Prevent disease
- Coping with illness and disability
- Prevent burnout
- Improve your quality of life

SELF-CARE INCLUDES...

Why Is Self-Care Important?

Self-care diminishes the effects of negative emotions such as anxiety, stress, anger, and sadness. It aids in maintaining balance in our lives, fosters a sense of purpose and belonging, and encourages us to reach our life goals, ultimately enhancing our quality of life.

Additionally, self-care can positively impact individuals with mental health disorders such as BPD, bipolar disorder, depression, anxiety, or stress.

> **EXERCISE 6.1:** My Self-Care Plan Template. As you read the circle, mark or make a note of what might apply to you or interest you in doing, saying, and acting following your benefit.

MY SELF-CARE PLAN

This is **your** Self-Care Plan Template. There are no right or wrong answers and no "perfect" way to complete it. You can express yourself through words, pictures, links, or other creative means. Be true to yourself and identify what feels right for you now. Remember, you can always change your mind and adjust your plan! This document is evolving and flexible, serving as a starting point. It is your commitment to prioritize your health and well-being throughout your journey.

Created by: Judy Be Well

Date: 03/25/2025

How do you know when you are stressed and need to practice extra self-care? What are the signs?

1. Begin to get numb/want to run/not feel
2. Begin to get very irritated
3. Begin to get anxiety symptoms, like worrying, obsessing

Take some time to think about your current self-care. What do you currently do?

The Whole Person Model

Mind	Body
Current Practices: 1. Distract myself with tv/movies 2. Create art/do a hobby 3. Listen to music 4. Research	Current Practices: 1. Stretching 2. Deep breathing 3. Go for a walk 4. Take a nap

Social or Cultural	Spirit
Current Practices: 1. Talk with a friend 2. Go out for coffee 3. Play board games with the kids 4. Support group	Current Practices: 1. Meditate 2. Volunteer/help someone 3. Relax 4. Practice mindfulness

Identify new, quick, and easy practices to try for each area (examples are provided below; feel free to use these examples and develop your own!). Additionally, you can create a vision board using the concepts and boxes below as a general guide for the organization.

Mind (e.g., watching a comedy on TV or reading a book)	Body (e.g., going for a short walk or dancing in the living room)
New Practices: 1. Create a new playlist Plan goals/life visions 2. Go to the art museum/museum 3. Research a new subject 4. Take pictures of interesting things 5. Declutter living room	New Practices: 1. Go for regular walks 2. Yoga 3. Get a massage 4. Jump rope 5. Take a hot shower 6. Eat well
Social or Cultural (e.g., game night with your kids or calling a friend)	Spirit (e.g., closing your eyes for 2 minutes and breathing deeply, or listening to your favorite music)
New Practices: 1. Call a friend just to say hi 2. Cuddle with someone 3. Be around people 4. Be nice to people 5. Join a new support group	New Practices: 1. Pray 2. Turn the other cheek 3. Spiritual journal 4. Practice empathy and compassion 5. Study virtues/practice them 6. Be kind/do nice things 7. Gratitude journal 8. Practice mindfulness

Identify three people you can call or visit to talk about your thoughts and feelings:

1. Melanie
2. Johnny
3. Amanda

Identify three positive statements, motivational quotes, images, or links to videos that reflect your strengths (e.g., "I know I am strong enough to achieve this goal," or listing your strengths from your VIA Survey of Character Strengths).

- √ "Stop letting it bother you; just let it go. Your mind can only take so much."
- √ "Life is short: break the rules, forgive quickly, kiss slowly, love truly, laugh uncontrollably, and never regret anything that made you smile."
- √ "Always choose the option that scares you the most, because that's the one that will help you grow."
- √ "Accept what is, let go of what was, and have faith in what will be."
- √ "When it's real, you can't just walk away."
- √ "I was created for a purpose."

What are your triggers you will work on?

1. My mom
2. When the kids are crazy
3. Not enough sleep
4. Fear my boyfriend will leave me

SELF-CARE CONTRACT: If I notice any of the following signs or symptoms of stress, I commit to finding time to take my good advice. I will avoid doing the following:

1. Being around toxic people
2. Not going to my therapy appointments

Instead, I am committed to caring for myself and nurturing my well-being by engaging in the following activities, behaviors, or actions, keeping in mind that I need to care for my mind, body, social and cultural self, and spirit (list at least three, but feel free to list as many as you like):

1. Take a nap
2. Research a new subject
3. Talk to a friend
4. Write poetry
5. Laugh (stand-up comedies)
6. Meditate
7. Learn something new
8. Make a to-do list
9. Go for regular walks
10. Get outside
11. Take a hot shower
12. Use positive self-talk
13. Read a book
14. Think positively
15. Journal
16. Forgive others and myself

17. Deep breathing
18. Practice mindfulness
19. Listen to upbeat music
20. Recite affirmations
21. Volunteer
22. Pet the cats
23. Yoga
24. Go up and down stairs
25. Sing
26. Take a 10-minute nap
27. Aromatherapy

I will reach out to one of the following individuals to discuss my feelings and thoughts:

1. Jeremy
2. My therapist
3. My friends

Signature: **Date:**

EXERCISE 6.2: This is **your** Self-Care Plan form. There are no right or wrong answers and no "perfect" way to complete it—you can use words, pictures, links, or other creative methods. Be authentic and determine what is right for you currently. Remember that you can always change your mind and adjust your plan! This document is evolving and flexible—it's a place to start. This is your commitment to prioritize your health and well-being throughout the journey.

MY SELF-CARE PLAN FORM

Created by: Date:

How do you know when you are stressed and need to practice extra self-care? What are at least three signs?

1.

2.

Take some time to think about your current self-care. What do you currently do?

Mind	Body
Current Practices:	Current Practices:
Social or Cultural	Spirit
Current Practices:	Current Practices:

Identify new, quick, and straightforward practices you might consider trying for each area (examples are provided below; feel free to use these examples but also come up with your own!). If you'd like, you can create a vision board using the concepts and boxes below as a general organizational guide.

Mind (e.g., watching a comedy on TV or reading a book) New Practices:	**Body** (e.g., going for a short walk or dancing in the living room) New Practices:
Social or Cultural (e.g., game night with your kids or calling a friend) New Practices:	**Spirit** (e.g., closing your eyes for 2 minutes and breathing deeply, or listening to your favorite music) New Practices:

Identify three people you can call or visit to talk about your thoughts and feelings:

1.

2.

3.

Do you have any co-dependent or what you consider "toxic" or unhealthy relationships? State the person's first initial only. Then, briefly describe your experience with that person and why it's toxic. Then, state the boundaries that are necessary to retain this/these relationships.

Identify three affirmative statements, inspirational quotes, images, or links to videos that remind you of your strengths (e.g., "I know I am strong enough to accomplish this goal," or listing your strengths from your VIA Survey of Character Strengths)

More think about triggers. (1) Sum up each trigger in a few words; (2) then state why you think it is a trigger; (3) What specific response occurs when you confront a trigger?

1.

2.

3.

1.

2.

3.

1.

2.

3.

1.

2.

3.

Do you engage in any self-destructive behaviors or activities? Examples might include doing any non-prescription medications, drugs, cutting, purging, etc. What triggers you to engage in the behavior?

If I notice any of the following signs or symptoms of stress, I commit to finding time to take my good advice. I will avoid doing the following:

CONTRACT WITH SELF

I promise to follow through on, amend, and revise my Self-Care and Trigger Plans. I commit to taking care of myself and nurturing my well-being by enacting the lessons I found helpful in this workbook, keeping in mind that my mind, body, socio-cultural self, and spirit must be cared for.

I will contact one of the following people to talk to them about my feelings and thoughts:
1. My
2. My

I will review the following to remind me of my strengths:
1. My
2. My

Signature: Date:

SELF-CARE IS NECESSARY TO WELL-BEING AND HAPPINESS

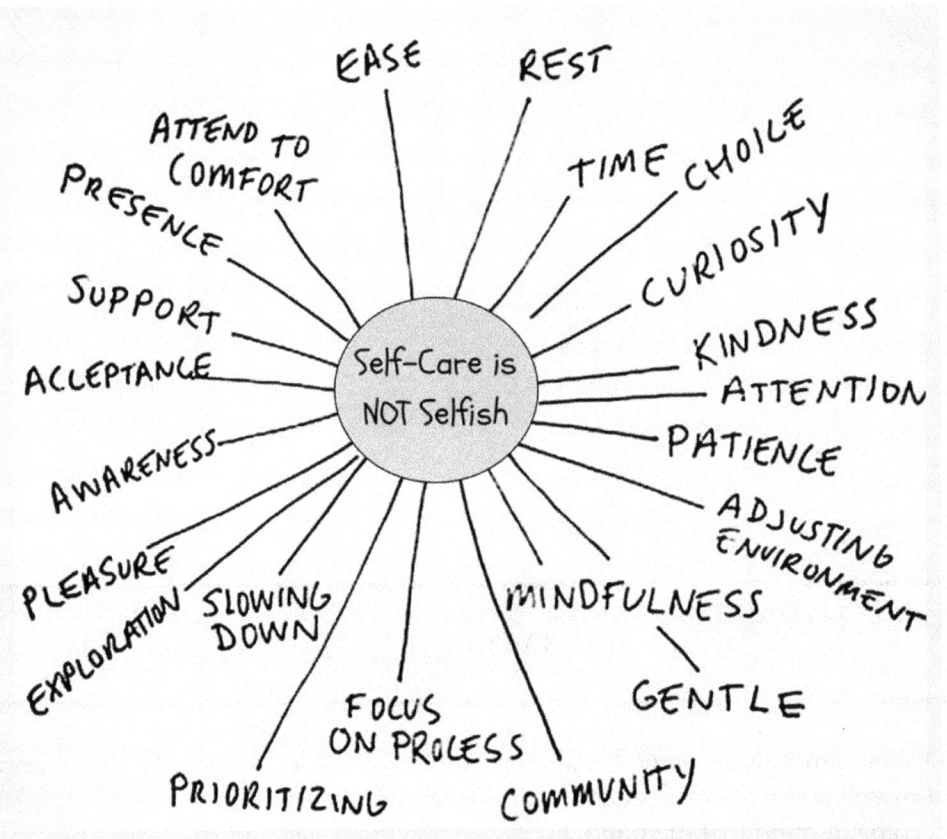

Olivia's Story

I'm Olivia, and I want to share my experiences, both good and bad, with borderline personality disorder, depression, and alcohol dependence. Due to childhood traumas, at the age of 17, I began experimenting with alcohol to relax and have fun. As time went on, I started drinking more and trying different mixed drinks. During this period, my BPD symptoms intensified alongside my alcohol use.

I dropped out of college, spending nights in clubs and pubs while sleeping during the day. The romantic relationship I had at that time was far from healthy—both of us drank, gambled, and argued frequently. It even escalated to not just verbal but also physical abuse, which ultimately ended badly.

Afterward, I went through some breakups with this guy, which affected me significantly. I lost weight, stopped eating, continued drinking, and couldn't sleep. Worst of all, I entered another chaotic phase of my life—sexual relationships with different people, seeking superficial connections but wanting more. I became attached to these guys, offered myself to them, and after three days, two weeks, or a month, I felt like I didn't belong to them.

I honestly struggled and became desperate, voluntarily visiting a psychiatrist for the first time while grappling with suicidal thoughts, alcohol use, and periods of sadness lasting for months. I was recommended for treatment. I was stable for only two or three months, after which I began drinking again.

In November, I found myself in the emergency room due to suicidal thoughts. I laughed at the wall, talked to it, and then cried. I stuck to treatment more closely, but I still struggled with alcohol abuse; eventually, I managed to quit. I experienced two more admissions.

Although I continue to face challenges with alcohol, using certain substances, and neglecting my medication, with my emotions fluctuating like waves, I am determined to change this lifestyle that leads nowhere.

POSITIVE AFFIRMATIONS

Use present tense when constructing affirmations.

Positive Affirmation Cards

Positive affirmations for BPD emphasize acceptance, strength, and self-love. They also maintain a strong emotional focus, actively countering the intense mood swings and overwhelming feelings that define BPD.

They also help you, which is something we borderline individuals tend to do a lot because of fear and paranoia.

EXERCISE 6.3: Create your own Oracle deck of index cards

Using positive affirmations for BPD helps to calm my mind when I'm about to lose my head over something trivial (like an unanswered text or offhand comment). They help me to talk myself down from irrational, intense, and paranoid BPD thought loops, clearing my mind enough for me to rationalize and self-soothe.

Affirmations Deck Sample Cards

1. Live your best life.
2. Connect with people who will help you realize your potential.
3. Relax… slow down…
4. Take time to heal.
5. Stand tall.
6. You are badass!
7. You are unique.
8. Reflect on what makes you special.
9. You are okay.
10. Let it go.
11. Don't worry about it.
12. You are good.
13. Love yourself first.
14. Keep going. Don't give up.
15. You are a good person.
16. I am worthy of love.
17. I am resilient.
18. I'm a survivor.
19. I find meaning in life.
20. I am strong and resilient.
21. My future looks bright when I step back.
22. Be happy.

23. Are you upset?
24. It's okay to not be okay.
25. You are good enough.
26. You're not the problem.
27. Release your past burdens.
28. Confidence is the key to success.
29. You can achieve your goals.
30. You are deserving and loved.
31. I am in control of my emotions.
32. Forgive yourself for past mistakes.
33. You are tuned in.
34. Stay calm.
35. You are doing a great job managing your emotions.
36. I forgive myself for my past mistakes.
37. I am at home in my body.
38. What can I do?
39. I am stable and secure within myself.
40. I am stronger and more rational than my fears.
41. I am full of love and gratitude.
42. Pregnancy alert!!!
43. Time out.
44. I accept myself for who I am.
45. I am my own person, with a beautiful and unique identity.
46. I am not defined by my mental health challenges.
47. I can control how I respond to stressful situations.
48. My happiness comes from within.
49. This too shall pass.
50. Take a chill pill.
51. I am in full control of my body and refuse to succumb to anger.
52. I am independent.
53. I am a good person.
54. I am healing more and more every day.
55. I forgive everyone who hurt me and let them go with love.
56. BPD is a label, not a weakness.
57. There is no one more important than yourself.
58. Door to value.
59. You are strong.
60. What makes your heart sing?
61. What's blocking you?
62. Don't stick around if you feel unwanted

WRAPPING UP
Self-Discipline, Self-Control, and Self-Care

Self-discipline and self-control are key components of managing a mental illness. They involve consciously regulating one's thoughts, emotions, and behaviors, even when experiencing challenging symptoms, by setting goals, following through on commitments, and resisting impulsive actions that could worsen one's mental state. Essentially, this means actively choosing healthy coping mechanisms and sticking to a treatment plan despite internal struggle.

Self-control is the ability to refrain from doing something you shouldn't, while self-discipline is the ability to start and stick with something you should.

Self-control

- Involves stopping yourself from doing something you want to do, like eating dessert or hitting snooze
- Helps you avoid habits that bring temporary comfort, like smoking, drinking alcohol, or overeating
- Helps you manage your emotions and impulses

Self-discipline

- Involves starting and sticking with something you want to do, like going to the gym or meeting a deadline
- Helps you manage your thoughts, emotions, and behavior to achieve your goals
- Helps you break big tasks into smaller, more manageable chunks

Self-control and self-discipline are related, but they are not the same thing. You can use self-discipline to replace something good with something terrible that you're trying to avoid.
Tips for enhancing self-control and self-discipline: Set realistic goals, avoid labeling yourself, don't be too hard on yourself for setbacks, and consider when you're most likely to exercise self-control. Self-discipline is crucial for maintaining mental health stability because it allows you to effectively manage your emotions, impulses, and behaviors. It enables a more controlled response to stressors and challenges, leading to better coping mechanisms and greater well-being. It helps you regulate your emotions, make healthier decisions, and avoid impulsive actions that could negatively impact your mental state.
Key points about self-discipline and mental health:

- **Emotional regulation:**

    Self-discipline empowers you to pause and reflect before reacting to stressful situations, preventing impulsive behaviors that could worsen anxiety or anger.

- **Stress management:**

    By setting boundaries and sticking to routines, self-discipline can help you manage stress levels and avoid overwhelming situations.

- **Healthy habits:**

Maintaining a disciplined lifestyle, including regular exercise, sleep schedules, and nutritious eating, can significantly contribute to mental stability.

- **Positive self-esteem:**

    Achieving goals through self-discipline can boost your confidence and self-worth, improving your overall mood.

- **Improved decision-making:**

    When you practice self-discipline, you are less likely to make impulsive choices that could later lead to regret or negative consequences.

Is managing a mental illness "work"?

Yes, and it's work that pays! Managing a mental illness can be considered work, as it requires ongoing effort, active coping mechanisms, and consistent self-care to yield significant dividends. Self-care pays off, as it can enhance one's stability and help one lead a fulfilling life. Taking care of oneself is essential to managing any chronic health condition, and it is viewed as work. With proper treatment and support, most individuals with mental illness can effectively manage their symptoms and lead productive lives.

Key points to consider:

- **Active management:**

    Managing a mental illness often involves actively engaging in treatment plans, taking medications as prescribed, attending therapy sessions, practicing stress management techniques, and monitoring one's symptoms.

- **Impact on daily life:**

    Mental illness can significantly affect daily functioning, requiring adjustments to routines, work schedules, and social interactions to manage symptoms effectively.

- **Resilience building:**

    Successfully managing a mental illness often involves developing coping skills, building resilience to stress, and learning to adapt to challenges.

- **Importance of support:**
    A strong support system, including family, friends, and healthcare professionals, is crucial for effective mental health management.

Self-care is essential for mental health because it can help you manage stress, boost your mood, and improve your overall well-being. Self-care can also help you build resilience and adapt to changes.

LIFELINE TO IMMEDIATE HELP!

Suicide Prevention Lifeline
988

Warm Lines
These are peer-run organizations and may not be available 24/7.

Crisis Text Line
If you can't talk, text.

Samaritans NYC
1-212-673-3000

Veterans Crisis Line
1-800-273-8255 (Press 1) or text 838255

RAINN
Sexual assault hotline
1-800-656-4673

National Alliance on Mental Illness (NAMI) Crisis Text Line
Text 741741
Again, if you can't talk, text.

REFERENCES

Albrecht GL, Devlieger PJ. The disability paradox: a high quality of life against all odds. Soc Sci Med 1999; 48: 977–988.

American Psychiatric Association, DSM-5 Task Force. (2013). Diagnostic and statistical manual of mental disorders: DSM-5™ (5th ed.). American Psychiatric Publishing, Inc.

American Psychiatric Association. (n.d.). History of DSM. Retrieved December 10, 2019, from https://www.psychiatry.org/psychiatrists/practice/dsm/history-of-the-dsm

American Psychiatric Association, DSM-5 Task Force. (2013). Diagnostic and statistical manual of mental disorders: DSM-5™ (5th ed.). American Psychiatric Publishing, Inc.

Barile JP, Reeve B, Zack MM, Mitchell S, Kobau R, Cella D, Luncheon C, Wilder-Smith A, Thompson WW (2013). Monitoring Population Health for Healthy People 2020: Psychometric Properties of the NIH PROMIS Global Health, CDC Healthy Days, and Satisfaction with Life Instruments. Quality of Life Research 2013; 22:1201-11. doi: 10.1007/s11136-012-0246-z.

Camp, C., & Hubley, A. M. (1998). Assessment of Living Skills and Resources. *The Thirteenth Mental Measurements Yearbook.*

CDC. Measuring healthy days: population assessment of Health-Related Quality of Life. Atlanta, GA, 2000.

Cella, D., Yount, S., Rothrock, N., Gershon, R., Cook, K., Reeve, B., Ader, D., Fries, J. F., Bruce, B., Matthias, R., & on behalf of the PROMIS cooperative group. The Patient-Reported Outcomes Measurement Information System (PROMIS): Progress of an NIH Roadmap Cooperative Group during its first two years. Medical Care 2007; 45: S3-11.

Cella, D., Riley, W., Stone, A., Rothrock, N., Reeve, B., Yount, S., Amtmann, D., Bode, R., Buysse, D., Choi, S., Cook, K., DeVellis, R., DeWalt, D., Fries, J. F., Gershon, R., Hahn, E. A., Lai, J. S., Pilkonis, P., Revicki, D., Rose, M., Weifurt, K., Hays, R., & on behalf of the PROMIS Cooperative Group (2010). Initial adult health item banks and first wave testing of the Patient-Reported Outcomes Measurement Information System (PROMIS) Network: 2005-2008. Journal of Clinical Epidemiology, 2010; 63: 1179-1194.

Camp, C., & Hubley, A. M. (1998). Assessment of Living Skills and Resources. The Thirteenth Mental Measurements Yearbook.

Carter, G. L., Willcox, C. H., Lewin, T. J., Conrad, A. M., & Bendit, N. (2010). <u>Hunter DBT Project: A randomized controlled trial of dialectical behavior therapy in women with borderline personality disorder</u>. *Australian and New Zealand Journal of Psychiatry, 44*, 162-173.

Center for Substance Abuse Treatment. Substance Abuse Treatment and Domestic Violence. (1997). *Treatment Improvement Protocol (TIP) Series*, Number 25. DHHS Pub. No. (SMA) 97-3163. Washington, DC: U.S. Government Printing Office.

Center for Substance Abuse Treatment. Substance Abuse Treatment for Individuals with Child Abuse and Neglect Issues. Rockville (MD): Substance Abuse and Mental Health Services Administration (US); 2000. (Treatment Improvement Protocol (TIP) Series, No. 36.) Chapter

Clarkin, J. F., Levy, K. N., Lenzenweger, M. F., & Kernberg, O. F. (2007). Evaluating three treatments for borderline personality disorder: A multiwave study. American Journal of Psychiatry, 164, 922-928.

Golding, S. L. (1985). Suicide Probability Scale. The Ninth Mental Measurements Yearbook. DeWalt, D. A., Rothrock, N., Yount, S., & Stone, A. A. Evaluation of item candidates: The PROMIS qualitative item review. Medical Care, 2007; 45: S12-S21.

Diener, E., Lucas, R., Schimmack, U., & Helliwell, J. (2009). Well-Being for Public Policy. New York: Oxford University Press. Duffy, T., Haberstroh, S., & Trepal, H. (2016). Creative approaches in counseling and psychotherapy. In D. Capuzzi & M. D. Stauffer (Eds.), *Counseling and psychotherapy: Theories and interventions* (6th ed., pp. 445-468). Alexandria, VA: American Counseling Association.

Foucault, M. (2006). Madness and Civilization. Vintage Books.

Foucault, M. (2001). The order of things (2nd ed.). Routledge.

Foucault, Michel, 1926-1984. (1977). Discipline and punishment: the birth of the prison. New York: Pantheon Books.

Foucault, M. (1976). The archaeology of knowledge. New York: Harper & Row,

Foucault, M. (1973). The birth of the clinic: An archaeology of medical perception. London: Tavistock.

Hargett, B. A. (2020). Disparities in Behavioral Health Diagnoses: Considering Racial and Ethnic Youth Groups. North Carolina Medical Journal, 81(2), 126–129.

Hyman, S. E. (2010). The Diagnosis of Mental Disorders: The Problem of Reification. Annual Review of Clinical Psychology, 6, 155.

Hays, Ron D., et al. "Development of physical and mental health summary scores from the Patient-Reported Outcomes Measurement Information System (PROMIS) global items." Quality of Life Research 2009; 18: 873-880.

Healthy People 2020 Framework: The Vision, Mission, and Goals. Overarching Goals. Available at **http://healthypeople.gov/2020/Consortium/HP2020Framework.pdf [PDF - 254KB]**

Healthy People 2020: Information about Healthy People and Foundation Health Measures. Available at **http://healthypeople.gov/2020/about/QoLWBabout.aspx**.

Hoffman, L. (2009). Introduction to existential psychology in a cross-cultural context: An East-West dialogue. In L. Hoffman, M. Yang, F. Kaklauskas, & A. Chan (Eds.), *Existential psychology East-West* (pp. 1-68). Colorado Springs, CO: University of the Rockies.

Gardner, John. (1983). *The art of fiction*. Random House, Inc. Print.

Golding, S. L. (1985). Suicide Probability Scale. *The Ninth Mental Measurements Yearbook*.

Ferrans CE. Definitions and conceptual models of quality of life. In: Lipscomb J, Gotay CC, Snyder C, editors. Outcomes assessment in cancer. Cambridge, England: Cambridge University Press; 2005. p. 14–30.

Ferrans, C.E. Definitions and conceptual models of quality of life. In Lipscomb, J., Gotay, C.C., & Snyder, C. (Eds.), Outcomes assessment in cancer (pp. 14–30). Cambridge, England: Cambridge University Press; 2005.

Foucault, M. (2006). Madness and Civilization. Vintage Books.
Foucault, M. (2001). The order of things (2nd ed.). Routledge.

Foucault, Michel, 1926-1984. (1977). Discipline and punishment: the birth of the prison. New York: Pantheon Books.

Foucault, M. (1976). The archaeology of knowledge. New York: Harper & Row,

Foucault, M. (1973). The birth of the clinic: An archaeology of medical perception. London: Tavistock.

Galderisi, S., Heinz, A., Kastrup, M., Beezhold, J., & Sartorius, N. (2015). Toward a new definition of mental health. *World psychiatry: official journal of the World Psychiatric Association (WPA), 14*(2), 231–233. https://doi.org/10.1002/wps.20231

Golding, S. L. (1985). Suicide Probability Scale. *The Ninth Mental Measurements Yearbook.*

Hargett, B. A. (2020). Disparities in Behavioral Health Diagnoses: Considering Racial and Ethnic Youth Groups. North Carolina Medical Journal, 81(2), 126–129.

Hyman, S. E. (2010). The Diagnosis of Mental Disorders: The Problem of Reification. Annual Review of Clinical Psychology, 6, 155.

Juni, S., & Retzlaff, P. (2001). Personality Disorder Interview-IV: A Semistructured Interview for the Assessment of Personality Disorders. *The Fourteenth Mental Measurements Yearbook.*

Jung, C. G., Henderson, J. L., Franz, M.-L.., Jaffé, A., & Jacobi, J. (2013). *Man and his symbols.*

Kindig DA, Asada Y, Booske B. A population health framework for setting national and state health goals. JAMA 2008; 299(17):2081–2083.

Kobau R, Sniezek J, Zack MM, Lucas RE, Burns A. Assessment of well-being: An evaluation of well-being scales for public health and population estimates among U.S. adults. Health and Well-Being. 2010;2(3):272-297.

Krahn GL, Fujiura G, Drum CE, Cardinal BJ, Nosek MA; RRTC Expert Panel on Health Status Measurement. The dilemma of measuring perceived health status in the context of disability. Disability and Health Journal 2009; 2:49–56.

Lewis KL, et al. "Borderline Personality or Complex Posttraumatic Stress Disorder? An Update on the Controversy," *Harvard Review of Psychiatry* (Sept./Oct. 2009): Vol. 17, No. 5, pp. 322–28.

Lindstrom B, Eriksson M. Salutogenesis. J Epidemiol & Community Health. 2005; 59:240-242. Juni, S., & Retzlaff, P. (2001). Personality Disorder Interview-IV: A Semistructured Interview for Assessing Personality Disorders. *The Fourteenth Mental Measurements Yearbook.*

Linehan, MM, Korslund, KE, Harned, MS, Gallop, RJ, Lungu, A, Neacsiu, AD, et al. (2015). Dialectical behavior therapy for individuals at high risk of suicide with borderline personality disorder: A randomized clinical trial and component analysis. *JAMA Psychiatry, 72,* 475-482.

Linehan, M. M., Comtois, K. A., Murray, A. M., Brown, M. Z., Gallop, R. J., et al. (2006). Two-year randomized controlled trial and follow-up of DBT versus therapy by experts for suicidal behaviors and BPD. JAMA Psychiatry, 63, 757-766. Linehan, M. (1993). Cognitive-behavioral treatment of borderline personality disorder. New York: Guilford Press.

Linehan, MM, Korslund, KE, Harned, MS, Gallop, RJ, Lungu, A, Neacsiu, AD, et al. (2015). Dialectical behavior therapy for individuals at high suicide risk with borderline personality disorder: A randomized clinical trial and component analysis. JAMA Psychiatry, 72, 475-482.

Linehan, MM, McDavid, JD, Brown, MZ, Sayrs, JH, & Gallop, RJ (2008). Olanzapine plus dialectical behavior therapy for women with high irritability who meet the criteria for borderline personality disorder: A double-blind, placebo-controlled pilot study. Journal of Clinical Psychiatry, 69, 999-1005.

Linehan, MM, Comtois, KA, Murray, AM, Brown, MZ, Gallop, RJ, et al. (2006). Two-year randomized controlled trial and follow-up of DBT compared to therapy by experts for suicidal behaviors and BPD. JAMA Psychiatry, 63, 757-766.

Linehan, MM, Dimeff, LA, Reynolds, SK, Comtois, KA, Welch, SS, et al. (2002). Dialectical behavior therapy versus comprehensive validation therapy plus 12-step for treating opioid-dependent women with borderline personality disorder. Drug and Alcohol Dependence, 67, 13-26.

Linehan, MM, Schmidt, H, Dimeff, LA, Craft, JC, Kanter, J, & Comtois, KA (1999). Dialectical behavior therapy for patients with borderline personality disorder and drug dependence. American Journal of Addictions, 8 279-292.Linehan, MM, Heard, HL, & Armstrong, HE (1993). <u>Naturalistic follow-up of a behavioral treatment for chronically suicidal parasuicidal borderline patients</u>. *Archives of General Psychiatry, 50*, 971-974.

Linehan, M. M., Armstrong, H. E., Suarez, A., Allmon, D., & Heard, H. L. (1991). Cognitive-behavioral treatment of chronically parasuicidal borderline patients. Archives of General Psychiatry, 48, 1060-1064.

Marion E. Toscano & Elizabeth Maynard (2014). Understanding the Link: "Homosexuality," Gender Identity, and the DSM. Journal of LGBT Issues in Counseling, 8(3), 248-263.

May, R. (1992). The Cry for Myth. New York, NY: Delta.

McMain, S. F., Links, P. S., Gnam, W. H., Guimond, T., Cardish, R. J., Korman, L., & Streiner, D. L. (2009). A randomized trial of dialectical behavior therapy versus general psychiatric management for borderline personality disorder. American Journal of Psychiatry, 166, 1365-1374.

Miller, A., & Ward, R. N. (1997). The Drama of the Gifted Child: The Search for the True Self. New York: Basic Books.

101 Things to Do Other Than Self-Harm. Retrieved on January 1, 2025, https://www.hopeforbpd.com/borderline-personality-disorder-treatment/reasons-not-to-cut.

Powers, Y. O., & Kalodner, C. R. (2016). Cognitive-Behavioral Theories. In D. Capuzzi & M. D. Stauffer (Eds.), Counseling and Psychotherapy: Theories and Interventions (6th ed., pp. 227-252). Alexandria, VA: American Counseling Association.

Psychotherapy.net. (Producer). (1997a). Cognitive Behavioral Therapy with John Krumboltz [Video file]. Mill Valley, CA: Author.

Psychotherapy.net. (Producer). (2011). Narrative Family Therapy. [Video file]. Mill Valley, CA: Author.

Reeve, B. B., Hays, R. D., Bjorner, J. B., Cook, K. F., Crane, P. K., Teresi, J. A., Thissen, D., Revicki, D. A., Weiss, D. J., Hamleton, R. K., Liu, H., Gershon, R., Reise, S. P., Lai, J. S., Cella, D. (2007). Psychometric evaluation and calibration of health-related quality of life item banks. Medical Care, 45: S22-S31.

Saad, M., de Medeiros, R., & Mosini, A. C. (2017). Are We Ready for a True Biopsychosocial-Spiritual Model? The Many Meanings of "Spiritual." Medicines (Basel, Switzerland), 4(4), 79. https://doi.org/10.3390/medicines4040079

Safren, Steven A., and Tracey Rogers. "Cognitive-Behavioral Therapy with Gay, Lesbian, and Bisexual Clients." Journal of Clinical Psychology, vol. 57, no. 5, May 2001, pp. 629–643. EBSCOhost, doi:10.1002/jclp.1033.

Schwartz CE, Andresen EM, Nosek MA, Krahn GL; the RRTC Expert Panel on Health Status Measurement. Response Shift Theory: Important Implications for Measuring Quality of Life in People with Disabilities. Arch Phys Med Rehabil 2007; 88:529–536.

Spillers, C. (2007). An Existential Framework for Understanding the Counseling Needs of Clients. American Journal of Speech-Language Pathology, 16, 191-197.

Toscano, M. & Elizabeth Maynard (2014). Understanding the Link: "Homosexuality," Gender Identity, and the DSM, Journal of LGBT Issues in Counseling, 8:3, 248-263.

"Treating Borderline Personality Disorder.", Directed by Marsha M. Linehan. Produced by Kevin Dawkins. Guilford Publications, 1995. Alexander Street, https://video.alexanderstreet.com/watch/treating-borderline-personality-disorder.

West-Olatunji, A., & Rush-Ossenbeck, C. (2016). Constructivist theories: Solution-focused and narrative therapies. In D. Capuzzi & M. D. Stauffer (Eds.), *Counseling and psychotherapy: Theories and interventions* (6th ed., pp. 419-444). Alexandria, VA: American Counseling Association.

Whitfield, C.L. (1993). *Boundaries and Relationships: Knowing, Protecting, and Enjoying the Self*. Deerfield Beach, FL: Health Communications.

Whitman, W., & Basler, R. P. (1962). *Memoranda during the war: & Death of Abraham Lincoln*. Bloomington: Indiana University Press.

World Health Organization. WHO definition of health. Preamble to the Constitution of the World Health Organization as adopted by the International Health Conference, New York, June 19-22, 1946; signed on July 22, 1946, by the representatives of 61 states (Official Records of the World Health Organization, no. 2, p. 100) and entered into force on April 7, 1948. Available at **http://www.who.int/governance/eb/who_constitution_en.pdf [PDF - 335KB]**

World Health Organization. The World Health Organization Quality of Life assessment (WHOQOL): the World Health Organization position paper. Soc Sci Med 2005; 41(10): 1403–1409.

Yalom, I. (2009). Staring at the Sun: Overcoming the Terror of Death. San Francisco, CA: Jossey-Bass.

Yang, M. (2009). Existential Themes in the Parable of Jesus. In L. Hoffman, M. Yang, F. Kaklauskas, & A.

Chan (Eds.), Existential Psychology East-West (pp. 1-68). Colorado Springs, CO: University of the Rockies.

Zanarini, M.C. (2009). Psychotherapy of Borderline Personality Disorder. Acta Psychiatrica Scandinavica, 120(5), 373–377.

Winnicott, D.W. (1956). Primary Maternal Preoccupation, reprinted in (1958) Through Pediatrics to Psychoanalysis: Collected Papers. London: Tavistock Publications; reprinted in London: Karnac (1992).

Winnicott, D.W. (1960). Ego Distortions in Terms of True and False Self, reprinted in The Maturational Processes and the Facilitating Environment. London: Hogarth (1965).

Winnicott, D.W. (1971). Playing and Reality. London: Tavistock Publications; reprinted London: Routledge (1991). Chapter 7: Mirror-Role of Mother and Family in Child Development.

Safren, Steven A., and Tracey Rogers. "Cognitive-Behavioral Therapy with Gay, Lesbian, and Bisexual Clients." Journal of Clinical Psychology, vol. 57, no. 5, May 2001, pp. 629–643. EBSCOhost, doi:10.1002/jclp.1033.

Skodol, A. E., & Bender, D. S. (2003). Why Are Women Diagnosed with Borderline Personality Disorder More Than Men? The Psychiatric Quarterly, 74(4), 349–360.

Van den Bosch, L.M., Verheul, R., Schippers, G.M., & van den Brink, W. (2002). Dialectical Behavior Therapy for Borderline Patients with and without Substance Use Problems: Implementation and Long-Term Effects. Addictive Behaviors, 27, 911-923.

Verheul, R., van den Bosch, L.M., Koeter, M.W., De Ridder, M.A., Stijnen, T., et al. (2003). Dialectical Behavior Therapy for Women with Borderline Personality Disorder: A 12-Month, Randomized Clinical Trial in the Netherlands. British Journal of Psychiatry, 182 135-140.Skodol, A. E., & Bender, D. S. (2003). Why are women diagnosed borderline more than men?. *The Psychiatric Quarterly*, *74*(4), 349–360.

Zaccour, S. (2018). Crazy Women and Hysterical Mothers: The Gendered Use of Mental Health Labels in Custody Disputes. Canadian Journal of Family Law, *31*(1), 57–103.

Zanarini, M.C. "Psychotherapy of Borderline Personality Disorder," *Acta Psychiatrica Scandinavica* (Nov. 2009): Vol. 120, No. 5, pp. 373–77.

www.ingramcontent.com/pod-product-compliance
Lightning Source LLC
Chambersburg PA
CBHW081014040426
42444CB00014B/3203